AIDE-ING IN EDUCATION

Madeline Hunter

Sally Breit

TIP PUBLICATIONS

El Segundo, California

i

THEORY INTO PRACTICE PUBLICATIONS

Motivation Theory for Teachers
Reinforcement Theory for Teachers
Retention Theory for Teachers
Teach More—Faster!
Teach for Transfer

Additional Publications

Aide-ing in Education
Prescription For Improved Instruction
Improving Your Child's Behavior

Copyright ©1976 by Madeline Hunter
TIP Publications P.O. Box 514
El Segundo, California 90245

First Printing, January, 1976
Second Printing, November, 1976
Third Printing, January, 1978
Fourth Printing, August, 1978
Fifth Printing, June, 1979
Sixth Printing, January, 1980
Seventh Printing, December, 1980
Eighth Printing, April, 1982
Ninth Printing, October, 1983
Tenth Printing, December, 1984
Eleventh Printing, August, 1985

PRINTED IN THE UNITED STATES OF AMERICA

Dedicated to the Junior League of Los Angeles,
whose interest, participation and support
made this program possible.

FOREWORD

In 1972, we at the University Elementary School at UCLA put to test our feeling that the teacher who knew how to promote learning, was the most important school factor in a student's success. As we began to work with discouraged, dispairing inner city teachers using inservice designed to increase students' learning, we received an offer of help from the volunteers in School Alert, a project of the Junior League of Los Angeles.

"Thanks, but no thanks," was my not too encouraging response. "I would as soon have a pair of untrained hands in surgery as I would in a classroom."

"Train us then," was the undaunted reply of these dedicated young women. So I and they began a series of night seminars to transform willing learners into skilled paraprofessionals. We had the able assistance of Mrs. Sally Breit, Supervising Teacher at the University Elementary School who had a real commitment to aides/volunteers.

The results convinced us that, for too long, educators have ignored one of our richest educational resources, the lay person who is willing to commit the time and energy necessary to learn techniques which formerly have been the domain of the professional educator.

We experimented with teaching the psychological theory involved in motivation, reinforcement, practice and extending students' thinking, and found that our volunteers "took" to it like the proverbial duck to water. Their questions and interest forced us to articulate with precision and practicality some of the skills of successful teaching.

The result? After watching these young volunteers' performance, as an additional head and pair of trained hands in the classroom, we became convinced that their training and experience could be "packaged" for the nonprofessional who wished to contribute to the world of teachers and children who need "someone to help." Consequently, with the stimulation, interest and support of members of the Junior League, we developed a ten hour workshop designed to lay the foundation for sophisticated and productive "aide to education."

The content of this workshop is applicable to all learners regardless of age, grade level, school organization, ethnicity or socioeconomic level. There will be many things you wish to add which are specific to your own school: rules and regulations, location of materials, office procedures, etc. You know best whether those things should be added to these meetings or handled in a special meeting.

We hope that you, as we did, will experience a very real sense of satisfaction through the teaming of professional educators with interested and dedicated people in the community who have been trained to work in the classroom. Together, as teacher and aide/volunteer combine effort and knowledge, a richer and more successful education can be provided for children everywhere.

Madeline Hunter, Principal
University Elementary School
University of California, Los Angeles

TABLE OF CONTENTS

GENERAL INSTRUCTIONS
FOR GROUP LEADERS

The meeting plans suggested in this book are merely outlines of possibilities which you should tailor to meet the needs of your particular group.

Groups vary. Some participants prefer to sit and listen until they have sufficient information before they feel comfortable enough to ask questions or discuss the material. Other groups immediately begin raising questions and interacting vigorously with the leader and with each other. While the latter situation may be more reassuring to the leader, that group is not necessarily learning more nor will the participants make better aides/volunteers.

Many parts of the meeting plans are labeled "if appropriate." This means that the leader should decide whether or not to include this part for her particular group. Some groups like to check themselves with "tests," other groups are uncomfortable with this procedure. Some groups prefer the intimacy and opportunities of small group participation, other groups prefer a total class format with the comfort of each member participating only when desired.

It will be helpful to keep the following generalizations in mind as you work with *your* group.

1. The participants must have information *before* questions, discussion or small groups. Pooling ignorance only wastes time. Consequently, they must have read the material *or* seen the film *or* heard a presentation. Usually the leader needs to "prime the pump" with examples.

2. Avoid the "best" solution, always stressing the full range of alternatives: "That's one good possibility. If it doesn't work, what else might we try?" will stimulate seeking alternatives rather than trying to find the one best thing to do.

3. Prepare yourself beforehand with examples that have alternative solutions and which include many of the possibilities you are trying to teach. Stress flexibility of thinking that doesn't stop with one possibility but generates several alternatives. With each meeting plan, examples are given in this book but the best ones are those you have experienced yourself in the classroom. Those have real authenticity.

4. Remember, at the first meeting, people will be getting acquainted and learning what the workshop is about, so that meeting will not be as spontaneous and comfortable as the meetings that follow. Don't be discouraged if the first meeting seems a little "stiff."

5. Each group has some enthusiastic members who tend to dwell on personal matters or raise unrelated questions. Develop ways of dealing with these so everyone's dignity is maintained and no one feels "put down" but the group is refocused on the content to be learned. You will develop your own skill and style, but here are some suggestions:
   "Mrs. _____ has made that point very vivid to us" (referring to her personal problem) "Now let's look back at the principle she has been illustrating." (Going back to the content of the meeting.)

"That's an interesting observation, let's look at our outline to see where it would fit."

"Many of us have had the experience of Mrs. _____ describes, now let's translate it into what might happen in the classroom."

"That is certainly a matter of concern. We'll jot it down and refer the question to the principal for (s)he has the authority and information to deal with it." (The issue may be school related but inappropriate for discussion at your meeting. Examples of such issues are teacher personality, grading, textbooks, schedules, yard problems, etc.)

6. Constantly scan the group to make sure everyone has a chance to contribute. The timid member won't raise her hand very high or won't speak out unless she is called upon. The leader must be especially alert to any sign or movement which indicates a non-participating member would like to make a contribution. Frequent sweeps of your eyes around the group will act as your radar. At first this will feel artificial to you. Soon it will become automatic and you will be amazed at how sensitive you become to the feelings of each participant. In addition, each participant will realize you care how she feels and how she is reacting.

7. Emphasize the similarity of working with children at home and in school. Aides/volunteers increase skills when they use them with their own children. You will need to bring examples back to the classroom setting however for final emphasis.

8. Continually stress the training and competence of the principal and teachers. Emphasize that, because they have the responsibility for all students, they are the final decision makers in the school. The aides/volunteers are there to facilitate and augment those decisions and are welcome teammates. Frequently point out that professionals continually use the techniques the aides/volunteers are learning but teachers have automated them so they don't have to stop and think. While teachers may not use the same labels, they are doing the same things.

9. Systematically communicate with the principal and others responsible for the aide/volunteer program of the school. Those people can give you invaluable support and feedback for the improvement of the workshop.

10. Take time at each meeting to explain the home reading assignment from the books and materials. Stress that this will be helpful in learning more rapidly how to become a skilled aide/volunteer. Encourage participants to read the optional material each week, to practice their new skills on their children to increase their own children's learning. When it is appropriate, give examples of how you have used these skills in your family as well as in classrooms where you have worked. Use caution so you don't "over personalize" the meeting or monopolize the time.

11. Save a few minutes at the end of each meeting to summarize the content and restate the home reading and practice assignment. Send participants home with the "glow of having learned."

12. Plan to be available for a few minutes after each meeting to answer questions, chat with any participant who desires it, put away materials and make any necessary arrangements with school personnel for the next meeting.

PLANNING PRIOR TO WORKSHOP

Suggestions for School Co-ordinator or Group Leader*

1. Consult with principal.
   a. Determine whether there will be ten meetings lasting an hour or five meetings of two hours each. If the films are viewed on television, ten meetings usually are scheduled.
   b. Clear dates, times, and the room in which the workshop will be held.
   c. Make sure that the following equipment will be available on the morning the course begins and each day thereafter.
      Television set or 16 millimeter sound film projector and screen. Be sure there is someone who can run it.
      Chairs for participants. (tables are optional)
      Chalkboard, chalk and eraser.
      Notebooks, paper and pencils as needed for participants note taking.
      Tables as needed for projector, group leaders, coffee, etc.
2. Arrange to have coffee prepared and ready at the time you set.
3. At least a month before the course is to begin send out a letter to all parents via the children. (See sample letter on page 64 which you may wish to modify for your school.) Be sure to emphasize that the enrollment form must be returned so participants may be notified. You and the principal will need to determine whether participants are selected to be representative of the parent body or whether enrollment is on a first come first served basis. Limit your group to not more than 30 participants as a larger group does not permit free discussion. Additional groups may be scheduled later.
4. When the class is filled, or on designated date, notify participants by a form letter or phone call. If there were too many applicants, notify those who were not enrolled and let them know when the next workshop will be scheduled.
5. A week before the class begins send a reminder of day, time and place by children, phone or mail.
6. A couple of days before class begins make name tags. Don't do this too early as there are always last minute changes. A large tag which can be seen from a distance is effective in becoming acquainted. Participants should leave their name tags on a table at the end of each meeting so they will be available for the next session. This also serves as a way of taking attendance.
7. Type a list of names of participants and group leaders, providing addresses and phone numbers. Make copies and give one to each participant and to the principal.
8. Check with principal or teacher co-ordinator as to whether a bulletin to teachers should be distributed (sample on page 65) and how the participants will be assigned to classrooms. If this will be your responsibility a questionaire such as the sample on

---

*Developed by Beth Lowe, School Alert Chairman, Junior League of Los Angeles

page 12 should be filled out by participant. Teachers should be polled by you or teacher co-ordinator to determine their wishes.

9. Match participants' requests with teacher requests and make classroom assignments at a determined time. Keep a record of who is working where, and what day and what time. Give a copy to the principal.

10. To evaluate the success of the workshop, you will need to deliver evaluation forms to the participants and to the teachers who have participants in their rooms. (Sample forms on page 66 and 68.

11. Make plans to determine the need for subsequent meetings after the workshop is completed. Occasional "get togethers" promote good feelings as well as additional learning.

WELCOME BACK TO SCHOOL
MEETING PLAN*

OBJECTIVE

The aides/volunteers will become acquainted with each other and, after viewing the film "Welcome Back to School," discuss changes that have taken place in schools.

1. *Introduce principal and participants*

Large name cards, that can be seen from a distance, should be available before the meeting.**

At the beginning of the meeting (before the film is shown) the principal and the group leaders should be introduced. If time permits before the film is scheduled, participants should introduce themselves and indicate names and ages of children in the school. If there is not sufficient time, introductions should be completed after the film.

2. *View film "Welcome Back to School"*

If the film is not available, teach the content or have the participants read the section on page 7.

3. *Lead discussion*

Emphasize that changes have occurred in schools so students learn more. List on the chalkboard the three major changes mentioned in the film.   1. what is to be learned,   2. what the student will do to learn and,   3. what the teacher will do to help him. Usually the teacher will determine what is to be learned but the aide/volunteer will need to let the teacher know when the learning task is too easy or too difficult. Aides/volunteers will be concerned with what the student is doing to learn and what they will do to help him. These are the skills that participants will learn in this series of workshops.

Emphasize the contribution to be made to children's learning by *trained* volunteers and how important it is to learn ways to help students so they will learn faster and remember longer.

4. *Introduce plans for the workshop*   (This can be done before film is shown if there is time.)

The plan for the workshop should be explained.
   a. It will be necessary to begin promptly each week. Name cards will be the record of attendance and should be picked up at the beginning of each meeting and returned at the end of the meeting.
   b. Information will be given by a film.
   c. The film will be followed by discussion to clarify and extend the information.

---

*The first and second meeting of this series may be combined in a two hour meeting.

**A 2″ x 8″ strip of sturdy paper with the participants name written in large letters can be stapled to yarn or string and worn as a "necklace." These are easily seen from across the room and enable participants to address each other by name. Name cards also act as a record of attendance as they are picked up and turned in at each meeting.

d. The discussion will include examples of how to use this information to increase students' learning at school and at home.

e. Reading will be assigned each week from the book *Aide-ing in Education*. Books should be brought to class each week.

Forms to determine aides/volunteers interests and times of availability should be distributed and filled out. Sample form on page 12.

5. *Homework*

(The book *Aide-ing in Education* should be available to each participant.) Read the section "Welcome Back to School" page 7.

If time permits and this hasn't already been done, aides/volunteers can be taken on a tour of the school where important examples of educational changes are pointed out and key people are introduced.

The group leader should end the meeting with an expression of appreciation to the participants and indicate she is looking forward to seeing them again next week.

WELCOME BACK TO SCHOOL!

As a school aide or volunteer, you are a new and very welcome element in this complex process of education. You've all been here before as students, but like everything else, education has changed and it isn't just the way it was when you went to school. Some things are the same but other things have changed considerably. The reason those things have changed is that we've found better ways to do them—ways that help students learn more.

You are one of the things that has changed the school. A teacher used to be the only adult in a classroom. What she could do, got done. What she couldn't get to, because she didn't have enough hands or enough time and energy, was left undone. Now you're going to help her get more of those important things done.

Ways You Will Help

You will help the teacher in several ways. Both of you will do some housekeeping chores. Like your home, cupboards have to be cleaned, supplies obtained and things kept so they're always available for work. You will also do some clerical work, filing, typing, correcting and recording. You may be supervising some students when the teacher is working with others, as well as at times when they go to the yard, the library or the lunch area. Your most exciting responsibility will be when you are working with children to help them learn. You need to let the teacher know your special talents, hobbies or interests so you can use them to make the classroom richer.

Things You Will Learn

Another big change in school is that we used to think any extra pair of hands, whether they were trained or not, could help the teacher. Now we know that if those extra hands are guided by a head that has some special training for the job, all kinds of wonderful things can happen and students will learn more.

You probably already know how to do the housekeeping chores. The clerical jobs are easy to learn. Working with children, if it is done well, takes special skills which the teacher learned in her preparation for teaching and which you will learn in this workshop and from reading this book.

Most importantly, along with helping students' increase their learning you'll find yourself growing, learning and working productively with materials, ideas, students and teachers in a partnership you'll really enjoy.

You will begin by learning about some important principles of learning that will help you work more successfully with students. These very same principles are important to remember and are just as useful and effective as you interact with your own family and friends outside of school.

Successful teachers have always used these principles of learning but many teachers do it intuitively. As a result, often they cannot tell *you* how to use them. In that case, you have to try to imitate the things the teacher does which is not the easiest way to learn something new. In this book we will discuss these principles so you can learn them. You will find that you, like the teachers, have been using some of them intuitively. Talking about them and learning how they work will help you use them deliberately, with the result that students will learn faster and learn more. And that's what you and the teacher are working together to accomplish.

Decisions You Will Make

Let's begin by looking at three critical decisions that must be made to assist a child with learning.

1. What is to be learned?

All teaching begins with the decision about *what is to be learned*—the learning task. This decision must be made first because all future decisions depend on this one being made correctly. Is the student to add or multiply? Is he to learn to spell easy words or hard ones? Is he to read a simple book or a difficult one? Is he to write a sentence, a paragraph or a story?

When you went to school, this decision probably was made on the basis of your age or grade. Now we know this is not the best way to make that decision. The science of human learning has demonstrated that learning grows block on block like a brick wall. In order to know which brick to put on next, we must know which bricks are already in place and put the new brick on top of them. Not up in the air, not where bricks are already in place, but at the point where the bricks leave off and the building needs to begin.

It's the same with learning. No matter how old a student is or what grade he's in, he can learn only the next thing beyond what he already knows. If he can read a third grade book, he is ready to read a fourth grade book. If he can read only a first grade book, no matter how hard he tries he cannot read a fourth grade book until he has learned to read a second and third grade book.

This is also true in math. If he understands how to add and subtract, he is ready to multiply and divide. If he doesn't understand addition and subtraction, no amount of effort on his part (or yours!) will successfully accomplish division, until addition, subtraction and multiplication have been learned.

So the first decision in successful teaching is to find out what a student already knows and what he is ready to learn next because *that is the only thing he can learn*. Usually the teacher will make this decision but you must be on the alert to let her know if a student is having trouble because the learning task is too hard for him at this point, or if he's bored because the task is too easy for him, or if his difficulty is just because he's not really trying. If the job is too difficult, your letting the teacher know will help to get that job changed to one he can accomplish so he can build on his learning and eventually do the difficult one. If the job is too easy, the teacher can suggest a more stimulating one. If he's not trying, in this workshop you will learn about things you can do to encourage him to try harder.

2. What will the student do to learn?

The second decision to be made in successful teaching is determining what a student will actually do in order to learn material which is at the right level of difficulty. Often, you or the teacher explains something and the student listens and looks. He needs to listen and look at first but then he must *do* something to let you know he has heard and seen and, most importantly, that now he can do the work himself. For example, if you are helping him with reading, he must do something to let you know he has learned the words and

8

understands the meaning. He must read aloud *or* find certain words *or* answer questions *or* locate information. *What he does* tells you whether he has learned. You can't just show him or tell him and hope it "took." You must make sure he *does* something so you know he has accomplished that part and is ready to move on.

3. What will you do to help?

The third decision to be made in successful teaching is determining *what you will do to help* a student learn. If he is working on a task at the right level of difficulty for him, whether or not he is successful in accomplishing it depends more on you and his teacher than on any other factor. That's what makes your job so important and why it is necessary for you to learn to do the things that will help him.

Most of this workshop will be focused on those things you can do that will help him learn faster and remember longer. To do those things will require that you know certain principles of learning. Then you must decide how you will use that information to help a particular student at each point in his learning. We can't tell you the exact things to always do or never do. That's what makes teaching a difficult profession, for you must always take your cues from the learner with whom you are working and use your judgment together with the principles you will learn in this workshop and then decide what you should do. It's not easy but that's what makes a classroom one of the most exciting (and taxing!) places in the world.

Confidential Information

You and the teacher, in working together, will become a professional team. It is important to stress that professionals have information which is confidential and should not be discussed with people who have no professional use for that information. So remember that what you know about a child in school is not appropriate for discussion with anyone but that child's teacher and the principal or support staff of the school.

Let's Start

Now you're ready to learn those things which will not only be helpful at school, but will be helpful at home with your family and with your neighbors, friends and relatives. We'll begin with some ways to make school a more pleasant place, where what you do will help children learn and where they feel more valued and become more capable.

You will see films and read the material in this book. Then discussion about what you have learned will help you put those ideas into practice. You'll be amazed at how effective you will become in "aide-ing in education" at school and at home.

COMPETENCIES TO BE ACQUIRED
BY AIDES AND VOLUNTEERS

As a result of these workshop sessions, the aide/volunteer should acquire the competencies to increase learning and improve student behavior by the use of:

1. *Motivation.*   The aide/volunteer will:
   a. State six principles of motivation and give an example of the use and abuse of each.
   b. Plan ways to increase students' motivation to learn.
   c. Carry out those plans in the classroom.
   d. Evaluate the success of these plans and make modifications to improve them.
   e. Use motivation principles effectively in daily interaction with students.

2. *Reinforcement.*   The aide/volunteer will:
   a. State four principles of reinforcement and give an example of the use and abuse of each.
   b. Plan ways to improve students' behavior.
   c. Carry out those plans when working with students.
   d. Evaluate the success of those plans and make modification to improve them.
   e. Use positive and negative reinforcement effectively in daily interaction with students.

3. *Extending Thinking.*   The aide/volunteer will:
   a. State different levels of thinking and give an example of each.
   b. Apply those levels in planning follow-up questions and activities for a story.
   c. Demonstrate the ability to read a story to a group of children, a) holding their interest through the use of story reading skills, motivation and reinforcement theory and b) promoting their learning through questions and activities that extend thinking.
   d. Develop a file of stories with accompanying questions and activities.

4. *Practice.*   The aide/volunteer will:
   a. State the four questions to be considered in planning practice and give an example of the use and abuse of each.
   b. Design a practice session for a student.
   c. Carry out those plans in a practice session with a student.
   d. Evaluate the success of practice sessions and make modifications to improve them.
   e. Use principles of practice effectively in daily interaction with students.

5. *Retention* (optional).   The aide/volunteer will:
   a. State the five factors that promote retention and give an example of the use and abuse of each.
   b. Plan ways to incorporate those factors when working with students.
   c. Carry out those plans in the classroom.
   d. Evaluate the success of those plans and make modifications to improve them.

e. Use retention principles effectively in daily interaction with students.

6. **Assisting in the classroom.** The aide/volunteer will:
   a. Demonstrate competencies learned in this workshop when assisting in the classroom.

AIDE/VOLUNTEER QUESTIONNAIRE

Name _____

1. Are you presently working in a classroom? _____

   If so, which one? _____

   What day and what time? _____

   Do you wish to stay there? _____

2. Are you willing to work in any classroom where you are needed? _____

3. With what age children do you prefer to work? _____

4. How many days do you wish to work? _____

5. Which day or days and times do you prefer to work?

(1) _____ (2) _____ (3) _____

6. Do you have some special interests or particular skills you would like to use? _____

   _____

7. List the subjects in which you prefer to work. _____

   _____

MOTIVATION
MEETING PLAN

(Review and clarify content from previous meeting if appropriate)

OBJECTIVE
The aides/volunteers will state or list the six generalizations of motivation and discuss the use and abuse of each generalization in working with students.

1. *Introduce topic*
One of the most important factors in a student's successful learning is his motivation to learn, how hard he will try, how much effort he will put forth. Students come to us with different levels of motivation but what we do at school will affect how much they try and how hard they work.

We are going to view a film that will teach us six ways that we can increase a student's motivation to learn. These ways are neither good nor bad in themselves, it's how you use them that makes the difference. After watching the film see if you remember those six ways and we'll talk about how we can use each one as we work with students so they will be more motivated to learn.

2. *View film "Increasing Motivation"*
If the film is shown on television, suggest that participants may wish to jot down the six factors as they are introduced. If you are showing the film, you may wish to stop after each factor is introduced and have a short discussion for clarification. If the film is not available, teach the content or have participants read section on page 14 before the discussion.

3. *Lead discussion*
"What was one generalization we learned?" etc. List the six factors on the chalkboard and discuss use and abuse of each. Use many classroom examples, applying all six factors to each example so all possibilities are considered.

If appropriate have aides/volunteers list the six generalizations of motivation from memory then give or have them volunteer the answers so they can correct their own papers. Make sure you model the use of motivation theory as you accept and dignify as well as expand the responses of participants. End discussion with "The teacher can help you with this," etc.

4. *Assign homework*
Read the section on motivation on page 14.
Read *Motivation Theory for Teachers* if it is available.
Try these techniques with children at home and at school.

INCREASING MOTIVATION TO LEARN*

All of us are concerned with the lack of motivation of some learners. Now we can learn how to do something about it.

Motivation is a state *within* a learner in the same way that hunger is a feeling within a person. No one can *make* a person hungry, but one can arrange conditions (the sight and smell of delicious food, or not permitting a person to have food) which will increase the probability of that person becoming hungry.

It is the same with motivation. You cannot motivate a learner, but you can arrange conditions that will increase the probability of the motivation to learn becoming stronger.

There are all kinds of factors that influence motivation; the learner's parents, his previous teachers, the quality of his breakfast, whether or not his team won. You'll note that all of these "influences" have already happened and there is nothing that you can do to change those past events. You can explain motivation (or lack of it) by looking at the past, but if you want motivation to increase, you must focus on the present and make something happen *now* that will affect the student's intent to learn.

There are six factors which have a powerful effect on motivation: they are 1) concern, 2) feeling tone, 3) interest, 4) success, 5) knowledge of results and 6) extrinsic-intrinsic motivation. You can use each of these factors in a classroom.

1. *Concern.* Learners are motivated to do that which they're concerned about. "I don't care," can mean, "I won't try."

If concern is too high, it interferes with motivation because it may become "I'm afraid to try." Each of us has an optimal level of concern that motives us to greater effort and higher performance. The athlete performs well when he is concerned about excelling. Some people "go to pieces" when they become anxious or concerned. Those people function better with lower levels of concern.

Watch your learners to see what happens when you do something to raise their level of concern. Does "I will be there in three minutes to see how much you have done" spur on a reluctant learner or disable him with too much anxiety? There is no one right thing to do, it varies with each learner. Don't let a learner remain unconcerned. ("I missed them all again"—big joke!) On the other hand, reassure an over-anxious learner ("Don't worry if you missed some, we're all having trouble"). These decisions on your part are what make teaching a profession and "aide-ing" a job that requires skill.

2. *Feeling tone.* What you do can make the feeling tone of the learner pleasant, unpleasant or neutral. For example you can say:

"You write such interesting stories, I'm anxious to read this one."

"That story must be finished before you're excused for lunch."

"If you aren't finished, don't worry, there'll be plenty of time later."

The first statement generates pleasant feeling tone which should increase the motivation

---

*This is a brief summary of the content presented in *Motivation Theory for Teachers*. That book should be available as a reference, for examples, for extension of understanding and for application of these concepts.

of the learner to finish his story. The second statement expresses unpleasant feeling tone which also may increase the motivation of the learner to finish but it could have undesirable side effects (he learns to hate story writing). The third statement indicates neutral feeling tone which has little or no effect on motivation.

So, by all means, increase a student's motivation to learn by making school pleasant. If that doesn't work and you must become a little unpleasant, *make sure you return to pleasant feeling tone as soon as the learner has performed.* ("It's a really good story, Bill, I'm glad I insisted you stay to finish it.") Don't fall into the trap of delivering a "lecture" once the student has performed. ("It's about time you finished.") Leave him with a pleasant feeling so he'll want to "do it again." Neutral feeling tone is helpful when you decide "this is not the time" for you or that student. ("Let's skip it for now.")

3. *Interest.* It is obvious that we are more motivated to learn something that interests us. The important thing to remember is that interest, like reading, is learned, not something a student is born with. A skilled teacher, aide or volunteer can develop students' interest in two ways: a) by making the learning more meaningful to the learner; b) by making the learning vivid or different from what the student usually experiences or is expecting.

   a. All of us are interested in ourselves, so inclusion of something about the learner along with the content to be learned is meaningful and very interest evoking. ("Bill, suppose you made five home runs every day for six days. How many home runs would you have made?") Increase in motivation occurs if you place a new word to be learned in a sentence with the learner's name ("Bill *earned* five dollars by helping his father.") The possibilities are limited only by your creativity.
   b. A second way to generate interest is to do things in a different or novel way. Change some things in the classroom or bring in something different, use "pen names" in creative writing, make a puzzle or game out of a necessary drill. Your initiative and creativity will help you to make assignments more interesting. If the student is not interested, change something! Make sure, however, that most of your effort goes into teaching. Don't put so much of your time and energy into novel gimmicks that you haven't any time and energy left for helping the student *learn* once his interest is aroused.

4. *Success.* A learner's motivation increases as his success increases. When a teacher, aide or volunteer wonders, "Why doesn't Bill work on spelling, he knows he has trouble with it?" she has answered her own question. You can make a student's success more probable by setting the task at the right level of difficulty for him. Make sure that the assignment is not too difficult, students will give up. The ones for whom the assignment is too easy will quit of boredom. If, *with some effort,* a student can be successful, he's more motivated to try because he experiences and enjoys his own strength and competence. The skilled teacher has assignments of different degrees of difficulty for different children (not necessarily different for each child). Diagnosis of learners, to be sure they're working at the right level of difficulty, and the use of principles of learning discussed in this book will enable each learner to become more successful.

5. *Knowledge of Results.* The answer to "How am I doing?" is highly motivational, for it lets a learner know when he's right or if he isn't, what he needs to change. He needs this information *while* he's learning—not the next day, the next week, or at the end of the year. When you check work, comments are much more effective in increasing motivation than are grades. "A good beginning, can you make the ending as exciting?" gives a learner a lot more knowledge of results than the grade of "B."

Having a learner check his answers as he's doing the assignment or immediately after he's finished, increases his motivation when he's successful and also builds in correction at the crucial time if he's having trouble. The most effective learning is accomplished when you make sure that the student knows when he has done well or, when he hasn't, what needs to be corrected. This is true in learning new patterns of behavior as well as in academic learning. Examples of giving a student knowledge of results might be:

"Tom, you did a great job of starting to work, now you need to let me know when you've finished the first part."

"Sally, you really played well today, you're learning to be a good sport."

"Put your thumb up if what I say is something that could have really happened in the story. You're right!"

Often you need to ask the learners to evaluate their own performance and answer the question for themselves "Today, how did I do on this job?" This encourages the more intrinsic motivation of the learner supplying his own knowledge of results.

6. *Intrinsic vs. Extrinsic Motivation.* Intrinsic motivation is developed when the activity or learning itself is the reward for effort. Extrinsic motivation exists when the student makes an effort to learn in order to gain something else such as status, approval, grades, to get it over with, or to avoid unpleasant consequences. Don't expect your learners to always learn only for the joy of learning. While that may be educational Utopia, we seldom achieve it. You and I are not intrinsically motivated to do dishes or get up in the morning, and there's very little intrinsic motivation in our aide-ing/volunteering when we're tired on a windy rainy Friday afternoon.

The more a learner is interested and successful with his learning, the more the process of learning will become it's own reward. In the meantime, use extrinsic motivators which build self-concept and a feeling of competence such as, "You did a great job, you should be proud of yourself," "Let's see how much better you can do today than you did last week," (rather than competing with someone else), recording new words so a student can see how many he has learned, a complimentary note to take home. All of these are more productive and emotionally healthful motivators than report cards, charts where everyone's scores are exposed or odious comparisons between students of different abilities. "You did that so well you should feel very good about yourself" is a productive and well deserved reward for performance.

Use all six factors (concern, feeling tone, interest, success, knowledge of results, and extrinsic-intrinsic motivation) as you work with students. Your own motivation in aide-ing/ volunteering will increase as you see how successful those students become.

For more information on motivation:

Hunter, Madeline. *Motivation Theory for Teachers*. TIP Publications, P.O. Box 514, El Segundo, California 90245, 1967. 43 pp.

Hunter, Madeline. Part II "Motivation Theory for Teachers." (28 minute filmed lecture) Special Purpose Films, 26740 Latigo Shore Drive, Malibu, California 90265.

DO'S AND DON'TS IN USING MOTIVATION THEORY

1. Do build a learner's productive concern about his learning.

   "Let's see if you can beat your yesterday's record."

   "I'll be back in a minute to see how you're doing."

   "We'll come back to it later to see if you remember."

2. Do use pleasant feeling tone.

   "I'll bet you can learn them."

   "You're really a fast learner."

   "You're fun to teach."

3. Do make examples interesting and meaningful.

   "Suppose you made five home runs everyday for four days, how many home runs would you have made?"

   "If you got $5 for your birthday and your grandmother said, I'll give you three times that much how much money would your grandmother give you?"

4. Do see that a learner experiences success.

   "Let's count how many new words you've learned."

   "You see you got them all right."

   "I just can't catch you."

5. Do give the learner specific knowledge of results.

   "Your spelling is correct but be careful your "i's" don't look like "e's.""

   "Your surprise ending made your story just great."

1. Don't build so much concern the learner can't concentrate on the task.

   "If you don't get them *all* right you'll have to stay after school."

   "This is the last chance you'll have for help."

   "Your whole grade depends on this."

2. Don't use pleasant feeling tone when it isn't working.

   "Even though you're not trying very hard, I'm here to help you."

3. Don't make things so vivid the learner thinks more about them than he does about the learning.

   "Suppose three monsters came in your room every night . . ."

   "Suppose you got three times $5 from your grandmother, what are all the things you'd like to buy?"

   "I'll time you with this stopwatch. Have you ever seen a stopwatch work?"

4. Don't have the job so hard he can't possibly do it or so easy he doesn't have to try.

   "I know you've never done one this hard but try to figure it out."

   "You always get these right. Let's do them again."

5. Don't give only general information.

   "That's o.k."

   "It's a "B" paper."

   "I put a check on your paper to show you I've seen it."

6. Do use extrinsic motivation when the learner has no intrinsic motivation to learn a particular thing. After successful learning many things become intrinsically motivated.

"Your dad will be surprised to find you know all this."

"Finish it so you can be one of the first out to recess."

6. Don't negotiate or bribe to get a child to learn.

"If you do this, I will . . ."
tempts him to consider whether it is worth it to put forth the effort. "Finish this so you can . . ." makes it clear the job is to be done but there will be pleasant consequences.

ADDITIONAL MOTIVATIONAL PHRASES

CONCERN

I'll help you with the first part and then I'll come back to see how you're doing.

As soon as you finish, you may go out for recess.

I saw what a good job you did in spelling yesterday, I know you will do well again today.

Good for you, I couldn't catch you on that page. Look at this next page and I'll bet I still won't be able to catch you on any words.

You will need to listen carefully when I read this story so when I finish you will know the answer to some questions.

FEELING TONE

Pleasant:

You have done such a good job, let's put your paper on the bulletin board.

I am writing 'good thinking' on this paper because you have done so well.

Let's show this paper to your teacher so she can see how hard you worked, that's why you got all the answers correct.

Unpleasant:

I'll work with you during free choice time and see what's giving you trouble with your spelling.

You need to show that you can do that page without any more help.

You need to do these problems by yourself and then check with me so I know you've learned how.

If you waste time now, you'll need to finish during your playtime.

INTEREST

You like football, Joe, so tell me, if the home team made 2 touchdowns and a field goal, how many points would that be? The opponents made 1 touchdown and 2 field goals, how many points did they make? Who won? By how many points?

Let's take some of the words you're learning and use them as we write a story about YOU.

18

KNOWLEDGE OF RESULTS

You answered all the questions about the first half of the chapter correctly, but you will need to read the last half more carefully to correct the answers to these questions.

You know all your addition facts but you still need to work on these subtraction facts.

Your spaces between words are too small. You need to make them bigger.

The paragraph you wrote was interesting, your choice of words good, the punctuation just right. Now you need to work on your handwriting so it will be easier to read.

SUCCESS

This whole list of words looks like a lot to learn, but if you work on just a few of the words each day you'll know them all by Friday. Let's mark off the words to learn each day.

You read that story with no mistakes. Here's a new book because you're ready for one that is more difficult.

Now I'll read a page. You be 'my teacher' and fill in the words when I stop.

EXTRINSIC

You need to learn your 6 times tables perfectly before you can work with that new_____.

When you've learned to work without disturbing the group, you may have free choice.

After you've finished, you may choose a partner and play this game.

Put a mark on this chart each time your math paper is finished on time. When you have 5 marks you may choose a special activity.

INTRINSIC

Yes, you may share your book on rock collecting that you enjoyed so much.

I see the subject was so interesting you read additional books beyond your assignment.

You're having fun making up your own problems in math, aren't you?

INCREASING PRODUCTIVE BEHAVIOR
MEETING PLAN*

(Review and clarify content from previous meeting if appropriate)

OBJECTIVE

The aides/volunteers will state or list the four generalizations of reinforcement theory, and discuss the use and abuse of each when working with students.

1. *Introduce topic*

Each of us *continues* to do those things that work out well for us or get us what we want. If we buy an inexpensive roast at a market and it is delicious, we go back to that market. If we go to a clothing store and get just what we want at the price we wanted to pay, we go back to that store. Whenever our actions get us what we need or desire, we "do it again."

Students do the same thing. They want to feel worthy, respected, that they are competent and are learning, so they will continue to do things that bring them these feelings. Consequently, at school, we can help a student learn faster as well as develop good attitudes and appropriate behavior when we let him know how well he is doing, how much he is learning, and that we respect him and the effort he is making. Psychologist call this strengthening of behaviors that get us what we want "reinforcement" of that behavior.

We are going to view a film that will show us effective ways to use reinforcement to help students learn. No one of these ways is right or wrong in itself. It's how you use them that makes the difference. After watching the film, see if you remember the four generalizations of reinforcement theory, then we'll talk about how we can use each one as we work with students so they learn faster and do better work.

2. *View film "Increasing Productive Behavior."*

If the group is watching the film on television, suggest that participants may wish to jot down the four generalizations as they are introduced. If you are showing the film you may wish to stop it after each generalization is presented and have a short discussion for clarification. If the film is not available, teach the content or have participants read the section on page 21 before the discussion.

3. *Lead discussion*

"What did we learn about positive reinforcement?" etc. List generalizations on the chalkboard and discuss use and abuse of each. Use many classroom examples.

If appropriate, have aides/volunteers list the four generalizations of reinforcement from memory. Then give them, or have them volunteer the generalizations so they can correct their own papers.

End discussion with "The teacher can help you with this," etc.

4. *Assign homework*

Read section on reinforcement on page 21.

Read *Reinforcement Theory for Teachers* if available.

Try these techniques with children at home and at school.

---

*This meeting may be combined with the next one in a two hour meeting.

INCREASING PRODUCTIVE BEHAVIOR*

Knowledge about and use of reinforcement theory contribute immeasurably to success in teaching, in a student's learning achievement as well as behavior. It is important to realize that reinforcement is always occuring. It is an integral part of human interaction and helps each of us learn productive behaviors. When we get satisfaction or recognition from doing something, our behavior is reinforced and we are more apt to "do it again." For the same reason, we go back to a restaurant where we have had a fine meal.

Due to lack of knowledge of reinforcement theory, and because it was first researched with animals (so was the Salk vaccine) some people have misinformation and believe it is a mechanistic or manipulative system. Nothing could be further from the truth. *Reinforcement theory is one of the most humanistic theories* for it accentuates the positive, building on a learner's strengths and ignoring as much as possible any undesirable aspects of his behavior. A teacher, aide or volunteer who uses reinforcement theory is constantly looking for productive behavior and strengthening it. As a result the classroom is a happier place for students and they are more successful.

The best reinforcers are those that build a student's feeling of worth and competence thereby enhancing self-concept. ("You're doing a great job, you should feel proud of yourself." "You're learning that very quickly." "That's good thinking." "You're really in charge of yourself to be able to ignore that.")

Reinforcement theory also is humanistic because, through its use, it becomes possible for *all learners to grow, improve and experience success.* Reinforcement may not be *the* most important theory in teaching but it is *one* of the most important. Clearly, it is also one of the most useful theories for it is used every day, every hour, in every classroom. Knowledge of reinforcement is equally useful outside of the classroom, for reinforcement occurs in our interactions with family, relatives, friends, professional associates, casual acquaintances, sales people, in short with every person with whom we come in contact.

Because reinforcement is always occurring, we need to understand how to use it so the results are productive for others as well as for us, rather than results being happenstance or even destructive.

Reinforcement theory is effective in the classroom in two ways:
    a. It strengthens productive behavior
    b. It can change nonproductive behavior to productive behavior.

There are four generalizations we must learn to apply in our use of reinforcement theory: positive reinforcement, extinction, negative reinforcement, and schedule of reinforcement.

POSITIVE REINFORCEMENT

A positive reinforcer is anything needed or desired by the learner.

When a behavior is *immediately* followed by a positive reinforcer, that behavior is strengthened and will occur more frequently. The immediacy of the reinforcer is important.
Most learners need or desire:

---

*This is a brief summary of the content presented in *Reinforcement Theory for Teachers*. That book should be available as a reference, for examples, for extension of understanding and for application of these concepts.

1. The approval of significant others (friends, parents, teachers.) When that approval builds feelings of worth and competence such reinforcers contribute to a healthy self-concept.

Examples:

"You did a good job of thinking to be able to figure that out by yourself."

"Your friends really like you because you're always fair."

2. Opportunities to do the things the learner enjoys.

Examples:

"You've done all your work correctly for four days, today you may choose whether you wish to do it or do something else." (Free time for having done a good job is a reinforcer to all of us.)

"You've demonstrated you know how to work independently, so you may choose what you'd like to do."

3. Special privileges.

Examples:

"You've worked so well, you may be excused early."

"You've shown me you know how to do . . . so you may choose whether or not you wish to practice when we work on it again.

Remember to reinforce students' productive behaviors (finishing work, trying hard, being polite, paying attention). Often these behaviors are taken for granted. When they are strengthened by positive reinforcement they become habitual.

Sometimes a person unintentionally strengthens an unproductive behavior by permitting that behavior to be followed by a positive reinforcer.

Examples:

A student whines to get his way and it works.

A student cheats on an exam and gets a good grade.

A student feigns illness and gets out of an unpleasant task.

A student uses rude or clowning behavior to get attention and he gets class or teacher attention.

EXTINCTION

A behavior is extinguished (or weakened) when that behavior is followed by no reinforcement whatsoever.

Examples:

The class ignores a silly remark made by a student.

The teacher seems not to have heard a request when it is made in an inappropriate way.

A child ignores teasing.

The teacher aide or volunteer must make every attempt not to have someone else reinforce the behavior she is seeking to extinguish. If parents are reinforcing unproductive behavior (whining, tantrums, avoidance of responsibility) the teacher attempts to enlist the parents' aid in a joint effort to extinguish the behavior. If this is not possible (and in some cases it isn't) that behavior can be extinguished at school but it will take longer. Students can learn that different behaviors work in different environments.

Extinction of *productive* behavior can occur if a teacher, aide or volunteer ignores the students who are doing the right thing and focuses only on the student who is out of order.

Extinction is not used correctly if a teacher continues to ignore a non-productive behavior when it is being positively reinforced by others. (The teacher ignores a smart remark that is made to get attention and the class laughs. The teacher ignores bullying but the other students give in to it.) Extinction is also being used incorrectly when a student is allowed to continue to practice a behavior which is unsafe for him or harmful to others. In these cases the teacher needs to use negative reinforcers. "You may not hit. If you're angry, come to me and I'll help, but if you hit you will have to leave the group."

NEGATIVE REINFORCEMENT

A negative reinforcer is something that is *not* needed or desired by the learner.

When a behavior is immediately followed by a negative reinforcer two things can happen.

1. A negative reinforcer is useful because the behavior that is immediately followed by a negative reinforcer is suppressed or "held back" (but not eliminated!). Suppressing undesirable behavior gives the teacher aide or volunteer time to TEACH a new and more productive behavior and follow that behavior with a positive reinforcer so the new behavior is strengthened.

Example:

A student says rudely, "Gimme that." The teacher responds, "When you ask me in that way I want to say 'no.' Ask me in a way that I'll want to say 'yes.' " When the student asks in a more appropriate way the teacher responds, (if possible) "Of course you may use it." If permission is not possible, the teacher reinforces the politeness by, "I certainly want to say 'yes' because of the way you asked, but it doesn't belong to me so this time I can't. You were really a good sport to be able to change the way you asked." (the positive reinforcer is the approval of the teacher)

2. A negative reinforcer can also be dangerous because *any behavior that removes the negative reinforcer is strengthened.*

Examples:

If not telling the truth takes away undesirable consequences, not telling the truth is strengthened.

If "getting a headache" excuses someone from cleanup, getting a headache is strengthened.

If crying takes away undesirable consequences, crying is strengthened.

If misbehaving gets a student sent out of a class he doesn't want to be in, or one for which he wasn't prepared, misbehavior is strengthened.

Note that a negative reinforcer signals a student what he should *not* do but it gives no information as to what he *should* do. Any behavior that takes away the negative reinforcer is the behavior that is strengthened. That is why it is essential that the productive behavior *be deliberately taught* and reinforced. By doing this, better behavior is learned by design instead of undesirable behavior by happenstance.

SCHEDULE OF REINFORCEMENT

A *regular* schedule of reinforcement, where the desirable behavior is reinforced every time it appears, results in fast learning.

Examples:

When a student is working on finishing his assignments, he should be positively reinforced every time he finishes one.

If a student is learning to make requests in a polite way, his requests should be granted every time it is possible. When it is not possible, he should receive approval or some other positive reinforcer for the way he asked.

But you don't have to keep this up forever, you soon change to an intermittent schedule.

An *intermittent* schedule of reinforcement, where behavior is reinforced one time and then not reinforced the next time, and the intervals between reinforcers become longer and longer, develops a very durable behavior that is long remembered.

Examples:

Once a student has learned to make requests in a polite way, the teacher will respond, "Not this time" or "It's Paul's turn." The next time he makes a request she will say, "Of course, because you always remember to ask politely." The next few times she will let fairness or the appropriateness of the request determine whether or not it is granted. She must remember, however, to occasionally reinforce the way the request is made so politeness becomes habitual.

After a student has learned to finish his work, the teacher will change to an intermittent schedule of reinforcement. At times the work is simply accepted but occasionally his finishing is reinforced by, "You really did that quickly" or "You always get your job done" or "I know I can depend on you to finish it so you don't need to have it checked unless you wish to."

It is essential that the teacher, aide or volunteer be consistent with reinforcers when a new behavior is being learned. If the old behavior is practiced on an intermittent schedule, and it works for the student, it becomes very resistant to change. It is equally important, once the new behavior is learned, that the teacher switch to an intermittent schedule so the new behavior becomes habitual and needs only an occasional reinforcer.

Because the teacher, aide or volunteer must reinforce newly learned behaviors on a regular schedule, only a few new behaviors (often only one) should be the subject for special focus. Otherwise it is impossible to monitor behavior and maintain a regular schedule of reinforcement. As a result of being over ambitious, and attempting to work on too many behaviors at one time, the adult can feel swamped and be tempted to give up, for she is faced with an impossible task.

It is wise to start with behaviors that are easier to change until the teacher, aide or volunteer develops skill with the conscious application of reinforcement theory. *Then* she can take on more difficult behavioral and learning problems. (The medical intern doesn't begin with a heart transplant.) Most students respond well to the productive use of reinforcement theory and achieve better self-concepts as their learning accelerates and their behavior improves. A few students have such severe problems that we can't hope to "cure" them completely, but they too will show some improvement.

The productive use of reinforcement theory results in positive reinforcement for the teacher, aide or volunteer as desirable results in student's learning and behavior are more predictably achieved.

Here are some steps to follow in changing behavior. Remember, it's always easier to talk about something than to bring it off successfully, so don't become discouraged when the first results are less than perfect.

1. Identify the *one* behavior that is to be improved or strengthened.
2. If a behavior is to be changed, identify the behavior that is to take its place.
3. Determine a positive reinforcer.
4. Determine whether to try extinction or whether a negative reinforcer will be needed, if so, identify one to be used.
5. Design a plan for getting the desirable behavior, so you have something to reinforce.
6. Put the plan into effect and set a time for evaluation to determine what modifications of the plan are needed.
7. Evaluate and make needed modifications.
8. Continue with the revised plan.

An excellent practice activity for the teacher/aide/volunteer that will yield classroom results is the selection of a common problem on which every adult in the classroom will focus reinforcement effort.

Remember that children will do well that which they are taught to do well. You can't expect them to do something well just because you've told them to, any more than you can expect a first grader to know how to read because his teacher told him he should. While learning to read, or to divide, or to play a game, or to behave appropriately seem very different, each needs deliberate teaching and help to correct errors at the time they are made. If this help is given, the learner becomes independent and reads well or divides correctly or plays productively without needing a teacher. This is the way all independent learning is achieved—not by admonition, but by teaching and reinforcing the students' efforts.

Don't expect overnight miracles but do expect surprising increases in pleasant feeling tones in your classroom and playground, increased learning achievement and better behavior as a result of your systematic and artistic use of reinforcement theory.

For more detailed information on reinforcement:

Reinforcement Theory for Teachers. Madeline Hunter. 1967 TIP Publications, P.O. Box 514, El Segundo, California 90245

Improving Your Child's Behavior. Madeline Hunter and Paul V. Carlson. 1971 TIP Publications, P.O. Box 514, El Segundo, California 90245

Translating Theory Into Classroom Practice: Part III "Reinforcement Theory for Teachers" Special Purpose Films, 26740 Latigo Shore Drive, Malibu, California 90265 (213) 457-7133

DO'S AND DON'TS IN USING
REINFORCEMENT THEORY

1. Do let a child know, when he is really trying, that what he is doing is worthy of note.

   "You remembered to put your name on your paper so I'd know whose good work it was."

   "You had a good game without a single argument. You're really learning to be in charge of yourself."

1. Don't be insincere or praise a child for things which are easy for him and take little or no effort on his part.

   "You did a good job of putting your name on the paper" (when he's been doing it for years).

2. Do let a child know he is making progress even though the work is not perfect.

   "That's getting better."

   "It's getting easier for you isn't it?"

   "That's coming."

   "Pretty soon you'll have it finished."

   "You're really trying hard."

2. Don't say something is really good when it isn't. Children usually know when something is not right and feel that praise for mediocre work is insincere.

   "That's great" (when he hasn't really tried).

   "You really know it" (when there are errors or halting responses).

3. When a child is learning something new or something that is hard for him, reinforce him for each part he does.

   "That's right, now what will you do?"

   "You did the first one right, now try the next one."

   "That's a good start, go ahead."

3. Don't wait until he is completely finished with a *difficult* task before you give him encouragement.

   "I won't look at it until you're through."

   "Let me see it after it's all finished."

4. Do vary the words you use.

   "That's just right."

   "You're absolutely correct."

   "You got them all."

   "That's excellent work."

4. Don't use the same word for everything.

   "Perfect, perfect."

   "Very good, very good."

   "Right, right, right."

5. Do follow a negative reinforcer with a positive one as soon as possible.

"Look at this one again. Good. I knew you'd find your mistake."

"Not quite, look carefully and you'll get it."

"Why am I stopping you from doing that? You're right, I knew you'd know."

5. Don't leave a child with a negative reinforcer.

"That's wrong."

"You missed five."

"No, that's not right."

6. Do ignore if possible, behavior that is merely attention getting.

Ignoring the "blurter outer" and calling on someone who raised his hand (if that's what you asked the students to do).

6. Don't make a "federal case" out of every little incident.

"Now just what did you mean by that remark?"

7. Do remember to reinforce every time when new behavior is being learned.

"That's great Bill, you always remember to wait until I call on you."

7. Don't be inconsistent with your reinforcement when *new* behavior is being learned.

"You didn't raise your hand and we'll listen to you just this once, but next time we won't."

8. Do be specific when you reinforce a behavior.

"Good job, you're finished right on time."

"Good for you, you remembered to come the first time I called you."

"That's just right, you have finished every problem on the page."

8. Don't be so general that the reinforcer is ineffective, ignored or "tuned out."

"Good."

"Great."

"Fine."

"Good for you."

9. Do state the reinforcer as a recognition of achieving the expectation that was set.

"Good for you, you remembered to come in and go right to work."

"You finished all those problems in time, just as you said you would."

9. Don't promote "teacher pleasing" with a reinforcer that is a personal value judgement.

"I like the way you came in and got right to work this morning."

"I'm pleased with you when you finish in time."

10. Do determine what is a positive reinforcer for each child or group.

If they enjoy a game, "You were such good helpers cleaning the room we'll take time for an extra inning in your baseball game."

If he wants teacher attention, say quietly to Jim as the group leaves for the play yard: "Jim, you were a good listener and remembered to raise your hand every time you had something to say."

"Jane, you listened so well during the story, you may choose someone to be your partner for leaders to the library."

10. Don't choose an inappropriate reinforcer for individuals or groups.

"Since you finished all the questions on this page, here's another set of questions you can do."

"Look at how straight Jim is sitting, ready to listen and discuss the story" (when the last thing Jim wants is to be the center of attention).

CLASSROOM APPLICATION OF MOTIVATION
AND REINFORCEMENT PRINCIPLES
MEETING PLAN

OBJECTIVE

The aide/volunteer will identify and discuss the principles of motivation and reinforcement in classroom episodes.

1. *Introduce topic*

Review the generalizations from motivation and reinforcement.

2. *View film "Motivation and Reinforcement in the Classroom"*

If the film is shown on television, suggest the participants may wish to jot down notes to help them recall examples. If you are showing the film you may wish to stop it to discuss episodes. If the film is not available, this meeting can be used to recall previous content and apply it to classroom situations or the group leader can schedule some "live" demonstrations of helping students.

3. *Lead discussion*

Discuss examples from the film and from participants' experience with using motivation and reinforcement theory at home or in the classroom. Make sure you model the use of motivation and reinforcement as you accept and dignify the contributions of participants.

Discuss and clarify additional examples. Encourage participants to volunteer classroom problems and apply what they have learned to develop possible solutions.

4. *Assign homework*

Encourage participants to re-read the material on motivation and reinforcement and to continue to practice these principles in the classroom and at home.

EXTENDING STUDENTS' THINKING
MEETING PLAN*

(Review and clarify content from previous meeting, if appropriate)

OBJECTIVE

The aides/volunteers will identify simple and more complex levels of thinking and design questions and/or activities at different levels of complexity as a follow-up to a story.

1. *Introduce topic*

An important skill of all teachers, aides and volunteers is the ability to select an appropriate story to be read aloud to children, to read that story well so it sustains interest and provides enjoyment and learning, and to follow-up the story with questions and/or activities that will heighten childrens' enjoyment and extend their thinking.

First, let's look at levels of thinking that go beyond just remembering or knowing about something. These levels have been organized by Dr. Benjamin Bloom of the University of Chicago into a taxonomy, which means a classification system. After looking at a film we will list some questions and activities at simpler levels of thinking and some that are more complex so they stretch students' thinking. We will be using this information in our story reading but you will find that it is just as useful when you are working with children in math, social studies or any other content area.

2. *View film "Extending Students' Thinking"*

If the film is shown on television, suggest that participants may wish to take notes. If you are showing the film, you may wish to stop after each level of thinking is introduced to have a short discussion. If the film is not available, teach the content or have the participants read the section on page 31.

3. *Lead discussion*

"What were the simpler levels of thinking? More complex?" It is not important to know exactly to which level a question belongs just as long as it extends beyond comprehension. "Let's do one together." (Take a story known by all. Red Riding Hood, Three Little Pigs, (see page 34) etc., or divide participants into small groups to list questions or activities.)

Report back to total group if participants have worked in small groups.

End discussion with "The teacher can help you with this," etc.

4. *Assign homework*

Read a story to your children at home and try encouraging them to do thinking at more complex levels.

Select a story to read to a group at school. List the follow-up questions and activities at simple and complex levels.

---

*This meeting may be combined with the next one in a two hour meeting.

EXTENDING STUDENTS' THINKING

Extending students' skills in complex thinking, as well as developing their ability to apply that thinking process to the creative solution of problems, has become an important goal of education. In spite of educators' dedication to this goal, many school assignments involve only recalling information and being tested for knowledge of facts (names, dates, number facts, etc.). Having information is important, but students need the opportunity, as well as the responsibility for using that information in life situations and in creative ways. Several years ago, Dr. Benjamin Bloom* of the University of Chicago developed a taxonomy or classification system of the cognitive domain in order to identify the levels of thinking demanded of students. This classification system makes it possible to deliberately develop school assignments and independent activities that enable students to practice extending their information into higher and more creative levels of thinking.

Bloom's six levels of cognition (thinking), *greatly simplified* are:

1. Knowledge: *Recall or location of information.*

This is the most common type of classroom assignment. An example of this level of thinking is the factual question (What did Columbus do? How much is 5 x 25? What happened in the story?). The information is remembered or the answer to the question can be located and does not need to be interpreted or inferred. Activities at this level provide the student with *information* which he can use in more complex thinking. There is nothing wrong with teaching facts, they are essential to all higher levels of thinking. But don't stop there, enable students to use those facts in more elaborate or creative ways.

2. *Comprehension or Understanding*

This level of thinking requires that students *understand* the facts they are learning, not merely recall or parrot information. "Why" and "how" questions may test understanding providing the student explains in his own words and doesn't merely repeat something he has read or heard. "Give an example" or "Say it in a different way" are ways of checking a student's understanding.

Examples of activities which require understanding are:

    a. Draw a picture that would go with the beginning of the story, one that would show what happened in the middle of the story and one that happened at the end.

    b. Give an example of something the boy did that showed he was dependable.

    c. Explain what you are doing while you are working the problem.

    d. How do you think the boy in the story felt? (Providing it doesn't tell this in the story.)

These first two levels of thinking, possession of information and understanding that information, constitute the foundation on which all complex thinking is built. A learner cannot do creative or high level thinking without this foundation. (For example, it is impossible to make judgements about democracy and socialism unless there is understanding of what each is.) The important function of teaching is to start with the foundation but encourage the student to build on his understanding and extend his thinking.

---

*Bloom, Benjamin S., ed. *Taxonomy of Educational Objectives, Handbook I: Cognitive Domain.* New York: Longmans, Green and Co., 1956. 207 pp.

3. *Application*

The third level of cognition is the beginning of creative thinking. Application includes activities where the student applies what he has learned to a situation which is new to him rather than one where he remembers the answers.

Examples of application activities are:

a. Solve word problems in math.

b. Apply a generalization or principle to a new situation. Examples: "Which of these imaginary animals could live in intense cold?" (Assuming that the student has learned that a warm blooded animal has to have some protective covering.) "On this map, locate the most likely places for cities." (The student had to apply what he has learned about the location of cities such as: close to a major trade route, where water is accessible, etc.).

c. Answer the questions: What might Goldilocks do if she came to your house and you weren't home? If you treated him as you would like to be treated, what would you do?

The ability to apply what has been learned to a new situation is a very important goal in education for we cannot possibly provide practice in all the situations the student will encounter throughout life.

4. *Analysis*

The fourth level of cognition requires that the student "take apart" his information to examine or work with the different parts. This level of thinking requires the ability to categorize, which is man's unique intellectual technique to reduce the complexity of his world. The ability to perceive similarity in different things and difference in similar things requires the skill of *analysis*.

Examples are:

a. Tell five ways the boy in the story is the same as you and five ways he is different.

b. List the words in the story that describe appearance and those that describe movement.

c. What were three main ideas of the story?

d. How was Magellan the same as an astronaut? How was he different?

When students have to examine information and assign it to a prescribed category, they are operating at the level of analysis. A higher level of thinking is required if they have to create new categories in order to organize the information. Creation or invention of new categories constitutes synthesis or the fifth level of cognition. An analogy would be the determination of where material belonged and filing of that material in an organized filing system (analysis) or the creation of a new filing system in order to organize the material. (synthesis)

5. *Synthesis*

This level of thinking requires that a student create or invent something; a generalization, picture, poem, story, organizational scheme, category, hypothesis. Synthesis requires the bringing together of more than one piece of information, idea, concept or set of skills.

Examples of activities requiring synthesis are:

a. A creative endeavor in the arts, a picture, a new melody, an additional stanza or a new poem or dance, etc.

b. Creating a story based on what might have happened if Red Riding Hood had met only a mouse in the forest.

c. Writing an original story.

d. Developing a hypothesis.

e. Designing an experiment that would test that hypothesis.

6. *Evaluation or Judgement*

Judgements are made when clearly there is more than one possible point of view. The difference between a judgement and a guess is that the student can give reasons to support the judgement he makes. This is the highest level of thinking because in an evaluative judgement or opinion there is no right or wrong answer until you consider the evidence that is used to support that answer or conclusion. A person's judgement is considered valid when there is evidence to support it. A judgement should be supported by the answer to "why do you think so?" or "how can you tell?"

Examples of activities on an evaluation or judgement level are:

a. Which would have been more difficult, to be Daniel Boone or Columbus? Why do you think so?

b. What should we serve at our party? Why?

c. Under what conditions might a person be justified in not telling the truth? Why?

d. Which solution is better? Why?

To ask learners to make judgements and support them with data is to require thinking on the highest level of cognition. To ask less is to deny students the opportunity to practice becoming intelligent decision makers.

These six categories of thinking (possession of information, comprehension, application, analysis, synthesis and evaluation) provide a framework for designing appropriate activities that extend students' thinking. Remember, however, that students must have information which they understand *before* they can use it in new and creative ways. A student can't be creative until he has acquired the skill or information necessary to that creativity.

It is not critical that you be able to identify or label the precise level of cognition for each learning activity. The important idea is to *stimulate students to think beyond recalling and understanding information*. Once those levels have been achieved, encourage students to use their information in problem solving and creative endeavors. Plan activities that require the student to identify similarities and differences, categorize information, speculate "what would happen if—," compare and contrast others to themselves, create a new beginning or ending. When you ask students to give an opinion or make a judgement about a person, situation or idea, have them cite the evidence which will support their judgement so it's not merely a haphazard guess or recall of something they have been told.

Make sure, however, that the student *has* the information necessary to do creative thinking. Do not ask him to give opinions about something he doesn't understand. Questions such as "Which is the better form of government?" "What do you think about this international crisis?" "What do you think about this political figure?" or other complex questions, may encourage him merely to parrot what he has heard from others when he does not have the information or understand it well enough to form his own "thinking opinion."

As you practice developing these activities for students, you'll be amazed and delighted to find how much you have extended your own thinking.

EXTENDING STUDENTS' THINKING
Sample Activities

Here are sample questions and activities for familiar stories. See if you can think of additional ones at the higher levels.

RED RIDING HOOD

Possession of Information
1. What did the wolf say his big eyes were for?
2. Where did she meet the wolf?

Comprehension
1. Tell what a hood is, in your own words.
2. What kind of a girl was Red Riding Hood?

Higher level thinking
1. What did Red Riding Hood's mother do that was kind?
2. Which parts of the story could have really happened?
3. Which parts are make believe?
4. What do you think the wolf would have done if grandma had not been sick?
5. How is Red Riding Hood's mother like yours? In what ways is she different?
6. Make a picture with one thing that is different from the story and we'll see if we're good enough detectives to find it.

THREE LITTLE PIGS

Possession of information
1. What did the pigs use to build houses?
2. What did the pigs say when the wolf wanted in?

Comprehension
1. How did they finally get rid of the wolf?
2. Why didn't the brick house blow down?

Higher level thinking
1. If there were no stove, what else might the third pig have used to get rid of the wolf?
2. How can you tell it's a make believe story?
3. Make up a story about another adventure with the three pigs.
4. Draw a picture about a different ending.
5. In what way is the Three Little Pigs like the story of Red Riding Hood?

THE STORY ABOUT PING
(Marjorie Flack and Kurt Wiese)

Possession of information
1. What did Ping and his family hunt for in the river?
2. What was the name of the river?
3. How did the boat master call the ducks at sundown?
4. What happened to the duck who was the last to get to the boat?

Comprehension
1. Why didn't Ping hear the boat master's call one evening? (more than one answer)
2. Why did the fishing birds wear metal rings around their necks?
3. Why did the little boy have a rope tied to the barrel on his back?
4. What time of day was it when the boy took Ping out of the basket? How do you know that?

Higher level thinking
1. What would you do if you were Ping and the last to get on the boat?
2. Ping couldn't hear the boat master's call because he had his mind on something more important to him. What might you have on your mind so you would not hear your mother or your teacher call you?
3. In the story what things did Ping do he should not have done? What are some things he did that he should have done?
4. List the things that made Ping unhappy.
5. Suppose the boy didn't help Ping escape from the basket, what different things might have happened to him?
6. Suppose Ping escaped and didn't find the Wise Eyed boat, what might have happened to him?
7. How do you think the boy felt when he let Ping go? Why?
8. Do you think the boy should have let Ping go? Why?

THE STORY OF COLUMBUS

Possession of Information
1. Where was Columbus going?
2. How did Columbus get the money for his voyage?

Comprehension
1. What did the sailors depend on to make their ships go?
2. What did they use to guide them on course?

Higher level thinking
1. List some of the things that would make a voyage difficult.
2. How did Columbus seek help when there was nothing he or the sailors could do?
3. When Columbus returned, how would the celebration be like one we might have for astronauts today? How would it be different?
4. What kind of a man do you think Columbus was and what makes you think so?
5. Who was braver, Columbus or an astronaut?

READING A STORY
MEETING PLAN

OBJECTIVE

The aides/volunteers will prepare a story to be read to children and design follow-up questions and/or activities at different levels of thinking.

1. *Introduce topic*

Reading a story to a group requires certain skills which can be learned Successful story reading results from the aide/volunteer having the skills to get the attention of the listeners and hold that attention by a vivid presentation of the story.

Today our workshop is planned to extend and sharpen your skills in the area of story reading. With this skill you can assume a teaching role with children. Students of all ages learn from hearing stories that are skillfully read. Also, you can free the teachers to work with individual children or small groups who require additional help.

2. *View film "Reading a Story to Extend Thinking"*

If group is watching the film on television, suggest that participants may wish to jot down particular questions or comments. If you are showing the film, you may wish to stop it for emphasis and discussion at certain points. If the film is not available the discussion leader should arrange for a demonstration of story reading.

3. *Lead discussion*

Discuss story reading skills demonstrated. Refer to page 37 in this book.

Discuss questions/follow-up activity in relation to extending students' thinking.

Identify examples of motivation, reinforcement, that the teacher used in the film.

End discussion with: "The teacher can suggest appropriate stories."

4. *Assign homework:*

(a) Select a story (from school or local library, classroom, home). Prepare it for oral reading with questions and follow-up activities.

(b) Optional assignment. (May come at later date so each aide can develop a file from the shared contributions.)

Each participant will summarize on ½ sheet of paper the story she has prepared.

Title

Author

One sentence summary of content

Students for whom appropriate

Follow-up questions and activities

READING A STORY

OBJECTIVE

The aide/volunteer will prepare a story to be read to children and design follow-up questions and/or activities which are at different levels of thinking.

Component Objectives: The aide/volunteer will:
A. Select an appropriate story using the following criteria:
1. Purpose of the story
   a. To teach
   b. To entertain
   c. To motivate, stimulate interest
2. Maturity level of children
3. Special interests of children
4. Background and experience of children
5. Size of pictures if shown while reading
B. Prepare for reading the story by:
1. Reading to become familiar with content
2. Practicing the story aloud.

(Optional activity: listening to tape recording of her own story reading to determine if voice has appropriate volume, variety of pitch, speed, and if voice is used to enhance story mood and character portrayal.)

3. Anticipating words and concepts needing explanation
4. Anticipating possible questions from children
5. Planning and preparing follow-up activities
   a. Questions to ask (Extending thinking page 31 as guide)
   b. Materials for writing or art activity related to story
   c. Directions needed by children in order to do follow-up
C. Read the story to children.
1. Sit where listeners can see pictures and reader's face
2. Set expectations for appropriate behavior
3. Gain attention of listeners with brief introduction
4. Read story
   a. Make frequent eye contact with listeners
   b. Move book so all can see pictures
   c. Help listeners to maintain attending behavior by using motivation and positive reinforcement
D. Present follow-up activity
1. Allow for stretch movement when needed
2. State expectations for how students are to respond to questions or participate in discussion
3. Ask questions or initiate discussion as planned

4. Give directions for follow-up activity
E. Dismiss children from story area avoiding "traffic jams" by first giving directions for dismissal and *then* dismissing individuals or small groups

Examples:
    a. Each child tells one thing about the story.
    b. Aide/volunteer dismisses children by saying letters of child's names, colors of clothing, eyes, hair, etc.
    c. Children sitting in back or side may be dismissed first to clear traffic lanes.
    d. "When you know you can walk quietly to your next activity, you may go."
    e. After planning with group and teaching children to do it, a child may dismiss individuals. (This frees adult to move to next activity and provides opportunity for each child to learn and use names of others.)

PRACTICE
MEETING PLAN*

(Review and clarify content from previous meeting if appropriate)

OBJECTIVE
The aide/volunteer will state or list four principles of effective practice and cite examples of use and abuse of each in the classroom.

1. *Introduce topic*
"Practice makes perfect" is not necessarily so. It depends on how you practice. First of all, the student must be able to attach meaning to what he is doing. For example, if he is working on multiplication facts, the aide/volunteer might introduce the practice period by "Suppose you liked a kind of candy that cost six cents. If you bought three pieces that would be 3 x 6 cents and you would multiply to find out how much money to pay. How much would that be?"

If new vocabulary is being learned, a student should know the meaning of the word and be able to use it in a sentence. Hearing it used by the aide/volunteer in a sentence with the student's name makes it easier to learn and remember the new word. Give examples such as "It took a lot of *courage* on Bill's part to volunteer to be the first speaker at the assembly.

Practice which is just "doing it again" is of little value. A student must have a real intention of *doing it better* and have ways of checking to see that he is improving.

There are four questions that must be answered in order to plan effective and efficient practice. In this meeting we'll learn to ask and answer those questions.

We are going to watch a film that will teach us those four important questions we must consider whenever we practice.

2. *View film "Improving Practice"*
If the film is shown on television, suggest that participants may wish to jot down the four questions as they are introduced. If you are showing the film, you may wish to stop it after each question is presented and have a short discussion for clarification. If the film is not available, teach the content or have the aides/volunteers read the section on practice in this book on page 41 before the discussion.

3. *Lead discussion*
On the chalkboard list the two words that emphasize each question being asked.
1. How much?
2. How long?
3. How often?
4. How well?

Ask the participants to give the generalization that answers the first question (a short amount that is meaningful). Ask group for examples (2-3 spelling words, 3-5 number facts,

---

*This meeting may be combined with the next one in a two hour meeting.

3 examples of interesting sentences to begin a story). If the group is not able to suggest examples, the discussion leader should have examples ready from her own experience or from the section on practice on page 83 in *Teach More-Faster!* Follow the same procedure for each question.

If there is time in this meeting, discuss the way to correct errors so the aide/volunteer "makes mistakes productive" as described on page 47. If there is not time, that section can be delayed until a subsequent meeting.

4. *Assign homework*
Read section on practice on page 41.
Read Helping in Reading, page 51.
Read Teach More-Faster! if it is available.
Try these techniques with children at home and at school.

EFFECTIVE PRACTICE

"Practice* makes perfect," is not necessarily so. Performance can be improved or it can become worse as the result of practice. It all depends on *how* a person practices. Sometimes there are ways of achieving effective learning with no practice whatsoever** and those ways should be considered before time is devoted to practice which is not necessary.

When we practice, there are basic principles that should guide our practice so significant improvement occurs with each practice period. As a result, not nearly so many practice periods will be needed. To achieve maximum learning gains with minimal time devoted to practice is one important goal of teaching.

There are four fundamental questions that must be considered before practice begins. They are:

1. How much of a task should be practiced in one practice period?
2. How long should that practice period be?
3. How close together should those practice periods be scheduled?
4. How will the learner know how well he is doing?

To answer each of those questions, we need to look at some basic principles that have been validated by research.

1. *How much of a task should be practiced in one practice period?*

The psychological generalization that guides our teaching decisions is: *the smallest amount of a task that retains maximum meaning is all that should be* practiced at one time.

Common sense would tell us this. We would not attempt to learn a long poem all at once. We would learn it one stanza at a time or even work on just a few lines of that stanza. Then after we knew those lines we would learn the next part. We would not hand a learner the 100 number facts and say, "Learn them!" First we would establish meaning so he understands what he is doing as he adds or multiplies, and then he would practice on only a few facts. After he learned those, he would learn some more.

While it seems obvious that we should practice a small amount that is meaningful, there are many violations of this principle. Teachers, aides and volunteers often attempt to teach, and students unsuccessfully attempt to learn, too much in one practice period. The result is a braid of confusion with frustration resulting from unsuccessful effort. Common examples of misuse of this principle of practice are:

a. Working on twenty spelling words in one period.
b. Studying all the number facts that have been missed (assuming that there are more than 3-5)
c. Trying to learn all about something (Magellan, the Civil War, the geography of a country) at one time.
d. Trying to learn everything that was missed on a test in one practice period.

---

*Practice is considered to be "doing it again" in about the same way.
**Teach More-Faster! Madeline Hunter. 1969. TIP Publications, P.O. Box 514 El Segundo, California 90245

The student and/or the teacher/aide/volunteer should select a *small meaningful part* of what is to be learned (the first half of the "five times tables," 2-5 spelling words, what Magellan did to get ready for his voyage, 2-5 things he missed on the test), learn those things, and then *stop* for awhile. Long practice periods usually are inefficient and often ineffective.

The more able learner can, of course, handle a greater amount (5-6 spelling words rather than 1-2) but he, too, should practice *intensively for a short period of time* and then stop for awhile. After a rest (which can be doing something related but not exactly the same as what he just practiced), he may resume practice to see if he remembers what he learned in his previous practice period. If he remembers that, he can add some new material. If he has forgotten some things, he should practice on those again for a short time and stop again for awhile.

2. *How long should each practice period be?*

The psychological generalization that guides our teaching is: *Short, intense highly motivated* practice periods produce more learning which is better remembered* than long, drawn out periods. Of course the period must be long enough to get something done but not so long that attention and effort wane from fatigue or loss of interest. It is amazing what a few minutes spent on highly motivated practice will produce in a student's learning and remembering. Short intense practice periods several times a day will produce more learning than double that amount of time at one sitting.

It is possible to expend too much time on ineffective or unmotivated practice. Common errors are:
    a. Writing a spelling word 20 times.
    b. Studying number facts for a half hour.
    c. Doing 30 examples to develop speed.
    d. Doing 25 of the same kind of problem.
    e. Going over the same thing for 20 minutes.

Obviously, the more complex the task, the longer it takes to do it. Practicing the writing of introductory paragraphs will take more time, even if you do only three of them, than the time needed to practice three spelling words. The length of the practice period must be tailored to the kind of task and the maturity of the learner. Highly skilled performers who spend many hours on practice, still practice intensively for short periods on only one thing.

It is helpful to see how much can be accomplished in five minutes of intense, highly motivated practice. For some tasks, 10–20 minutes may be necessary. If more time is needed, often it is better to break the task into parts each of which is practiced for a short period. Later when each part is learned, a longer period may be needed to put them together.

3. *How close together should practice periods be scheduled?*

The psychological generalization that guides our teaching is: Many practice periods close together should be scheduled at the beginning of learning. This *massing* of practice results in fast learning. Once something has been learned, practice periods should be scheduled farther and farther apart. This *distributing* of practice results in long retention of the material that

---

*Motivated practice is considered to be practice when the learner is really intending to improve, to "learn it" not just to "do it."

has been learned. When something new is introduced there should be several short practice periods within the hour (massing practice). Other short practice periods of the same material should occur during that day and on subsequent days. Once it is learned, a review once a week and then once a month (distributing practice) will more nearly ensure remembering. Here are some familiar violations of this principal.

    a. Taking a spelling test on Friday with no further attention to those words in subsequent weeks.

    b. Becoming familiar with an episode in history and then moving on, never reviewing or reconsidering that episode.

    c. Learning peoples names, and then not thinking of them again, so the names are forgotten.

    d. Reading a book or article, never reviewing what it was about, and soon you don't know.

Working on smaller amounts of a task in a short practice period insures massing of practice. For example, if a student is working on four number facts, each of those can be practiced many times (massed) in a one minute practice period. After they are learned, reviewing them twice a week, once a week and then once a month (distributed) will more nearly ensure their being remembered.

If a student misses something during a practice period he should come back to it again and again in a short period of time (mass practice). For example, if he is studying the last half of his 7 times tables and he misses 7×8, his practice should be: $7 \times 8 =$, $7 \times 6 =$, $7 \times 8 =$, $7 \times 7 =$, $7 \times 8 =$, $7 \times 9 =$, $7 \times 8 =$ until the answer to 7×8 is automatic. At his next practice period he should again check 7×8. If he knows it, only occasional repetitions are necessary. He should *not*, however, repeat the same response $7 \times 8 =$, $7 \times 8 =$, $7 \times 8 =$ without another number fact between each one. Repeating the same fact requires no thinking, just "parroting" which is ineffective for learning. He must always be making a "thinking, intention-of-learning" response.

When practicing reading it is important to mass practice on *any word missed.* Usually the student should reread the sentence that contains the word that was missed. At the end of the page he should go back to that word and read it again. If he doesn't remember it, he should reread the whole sentence for a clue. At the end of the story he should again read any words he missed to make sure he remembers them. It is helpful to make a list of missed words with the page number on which each word occurred, so the student can mass his practice by working on them several times that same day. The next day he should reread them and relearn any he has forgotten. If a student is missing more than 2-3 words on a page, that reading book is too hard for him (too much needs to be learned in one practice period). He should change to a book where it is possible for him to learn, each day, the words he doesn't know.

4. *How will the student know how well he is doing (knowledge of results)?*

Practice without feedback that lets the student know that he is right or, if he isn't, what is wrong, is seldom effective. The more immediate the knowledge of results, the easier it is for the student to improve his performance or correct errors. Consequently, the student must have access to knowledge of results either from written material or from a person.

In practicing sports, knowing where the ball landed, if the shot hit the target, how much time is being cut down in running, etc., are obvious necessities. Not so obvious, but equally important, is the information that tells the student how well he is doing in his classroom practice.

Frequent monitoring of students when they are practicing enables the adult to "spot check" and quickly identify any student who needs help. Such monitoring also gives successful students knowledge of results ("That's right," "You're getting them all," "That's coming along well").

A test becomes a highly motivated practice period when the student learns, as soon as possible after a test, what he got right and, if he misses something, what his answer should have been. Violations of the principle of knowledge of results occur when papers aren't checked or tests are returned after several weeks or not at all.

In summary, a great deal of learning time can be saved by applying four principles of effective practice.

1. Practice small meaningful parts and add more only after those have been learned.
2. Schedule short intense practice periods where the student is highly motivated to "do it better."
3. Mass practice periods at the beginning so the material is learned quickly. Then distribute practice so it is long remembered.
4. Enable the student to get knowledge of results while he is practicing or as soon as possible afterwards.

When you apply these principles, make sure the learner is doing the practice, not you; that *he* says the answer, *he* writes the words, *he* intends to learn rather than merely watching you do it or listening to you tell him about it.

Your job is to encourage him by helping him to be right, letting him know when he *is* right, helping him to realize *when* he has learned, *what* he has learned, and *what he still needs to practice*. Your support, approval and reinforcement will help him develop more confidence in himself so eventually he can become his own teacher and design his own practice periods—something he will need as an assist to learning throughout his life.

For additional information:

Hunter, Madeline. *Teach More-Faster.* TIP Publications, P.O. Box 514, El Segundo, California 90245

Hunter, Madeline. "Teach More-Faster." Part I, Part II, Part III. Special Purpose Films, 26740 Latigo Shore Drive, Malibu, California 90265.

DO'S AND DON'TS IN PRACTICE

1. Do work on short meaningful units.

   "Let's learn these 3 words."

   "Let's concentrate on your 8's."

   "What were the 2 words on this page that slowed you down?"

1. Don't work on a long unrelated series.

   "Let's work on all 10 of these words."

   "Let's work on the 100 multi-plication facts."

   "Let's work on all the new words in this story."

2. Do work for short concentrated periods.

   "Let's see how much you can get done in the next 5 minutes."

   "Let's see how many you can learn before recess."

2. Don't drag out practice periods.

   "Let's see how much you can learn by tomorrow."

   "I'll be here all morning to help you with your math."

3. Do review something a student learned when you previously worked with him.

   "Let's see if you remember your 8's."

   "Let's check the words you learned last time and then move on."

3. Don't skip an opportunity to review previously learned material.

   "You learned your 8's last week, let's move on to your 9's."

   "You learned 5 words yesterday, let's try 5 new words."

4. Do practice something new in many different contexts.

   "What two numbers will make 5? What other two numbers will make 5? What other two numbers, etc.?"

   "Use 'courageous' in a sentence that will help us know what it means. Can you think of another sentence? Use it in a still different sentence."

4. Don't practice something new only once.

   "What two numbers make 5? What two numbers make 6? What two numbers make 7?"

   "Use 'courageous' in a sentence. Use 'novel' in a sentence. Use 'mystery' in a sentence."

5. Do have a student practice something new several times while you are there.

"Now that you know that word, I will come back to see if you remember it in a few minutes."

"Tell me your new word before you go out for recess."

"Remember the word you told me just before recess, what was it? Good, I'll ask you again just before I leave."

5. Don't have a student learn something new and then not check to see that he remembers it.

"You learned a new word, be sure you remember it."

"Now that you've finished, we won't work on that anymore."

6. Do give a student knowledge of results.

"I'll nod my head each time you get it right. If I don't nod, you need to think again."

"As soon as you finish the first row, I'll check it and let you know how you've done."

"I'll go over your paper at noon so you can see how much you've learned."

6. Don't leave a student wondering how he did.

"A check on your paper means I've seen it."

"I'll return these papers after vacation."

"Just keep on practicing, it will be good for you."

MAKING MISTAKES PRODUCTIVE

A mistake productive? How could that be? A mistake is objective evidence that a student "doesn't know" or "can't do." A mistake alerts us to the fact that something needs to be learned. Without that mistake, the learner's problem might go undetected and therefore unremediated with the resultant possibility of more serious problems later on. A mistake uncorrected is the same as a mistake undetected, both could eventually swamp a learner. A productive mistake is one which is corrected and the right response learned thereby leaving the student stronger, with more confidence in his own ability and more ego strength to support him in the future mistakes which are inevitable.

When a learner makes a mistake there are two things he doesn't know. He doesn't know the answer to the question that was asked and he doesn't know the question to which his incorrect answer really belongs. If he says 5 x 8 = 45 he doesn't know the answer to 5 x 8 and he doesn't know the combination to which 45 is the right answer. If he says Lincoln was our first president, he doesn't know the name of our first president and he also doesn't know when Lincoln was president.

Both errors must be corrected. He has learned only half of what he needs to know when he learns that 5 x 8 = 40 or that Washington was our first president. He has corrected only half of his error. He also needs to learn that 45 is the answer to 5 x 9 and when Lincoln was president.

There are three steps in dealing productively with mistakes.

1. *Supplying the question to which his answer belongs.*

Usually the teacher/aide/volunteer should supply, in a way that is not demeaning, the question to which his answer belongs. "Forty-five would be the right answer if I had asked about 5 x 9. Now what would 5 x 8 be?" Supplying the question to which the learner's answer belongs not only gives needed information to the learner but maintains his dignity, feelings of worth and demonstrates he had important information, he just got it in the wrong place. To say, "You're wrong," or "That's not correct" makes even the most resilient learner feel embarrassed or foolish and such negative feelings should be avoided.

2. *Supplying Prompts.*

Prompts are questions or suggestions that point the learner toward the right answer. When he needs them, the teacher supplies prompts to help the student locate or figure out the answer. "If you bought eight nickel candy bars how much would you spend?" or "If you bought five nickel candy bars how much would that be? Six? Seven? Now eight? then how much is 5 x 8?" To prompt him on the first president the teacher might say, "Our national capital is named after him," or "His name begins with W."

3. *Checking to see that learning has occurred.*

The teacher/aide/volunteer should return to the same question before too much time has passed in order to check whether the student has remembered the corrections to both of his errors. "Now what is the answer to 5 x 8? And how much are 5 x 9? Good, now you know both of them!"

When a learner knows he is responsible for correcting his error, and that he will be checked as to whether or not he has remembered the answer, he is much more motivated to learn the correct response. Often the teacher can trigger his intent by, "I'll come back to you in a minute and then you'll get it just right."

Let's follow these three steps to correcting errors in our example of knowing the first president. The teacher might say, "Lincoln was certainly one of our most important presidents, but his term of office was during the Civil War." (Supplying the question to which his answer belongs.) "Will it help if I tell you our first president's name began with W?" (Prompts to help him generate the right answer.) If the student still doesn't know, the teacher or another student supplies the correct answer. There is no point in a student merely guessing when he doesn't have the information. *The teacher must then check to make sure the learner has heard the correct information.* "Now, what would you write in answer to the question, who was our first president? Good, now you know it."

We cannot assume that just because something has been said, it has been heard. Also students quickly learn that you are going to check, so they listen more carefully with an intent to remember. As one student remarked, "If you miss something in Miss Brown's class, she gives you a chance to learn it and you'd better listen 'cause, sure as heck, she'll ask you again before the end of the period!" (Checking to see if it has been learned and remembered.)

Let's look at a third example. A student has written "dessert" when he means "desert." The teacher might (1) say, "You wrote the word that means something good that you eat at the end of a meal, dessert." (Giving the question to which his answer belongs.) (2) "Do you know how to spell the word that means a hot, dry sandy land? What letter could you leave out and still have all the letter sounds you need?" (Prompts) (3) "Good, now whenever you spell it with two "S's," what will you mean? If you use just one "S" what will that word mean? I'll ask you again at the end of the period so you'll be sure to remember it from now on." (Checking to see if he remembers.)

In summary, students' mistakes are important signals that alert us to the fact that something is wrong. A mistake is destructive only if it remains uncorrected or results in a student losing confidence in himself as a learner. A mistake corrected by a teacher/aide/volunteer who is following these three principles can be an important assist to learning, both in terms of correction of misunderstood or unknown material, and in terms of the student's increased confidence in himself as a learner when he learns something he didn't know before.

HELPING IN MATHEMATICS
MEETING PLAN

(There will be no new content in this meeting in order to give participants an opportunity to refine and clarify their previous learning.)

OBJECTIVE

The aide/volunteer will identify and discuss principles of motivation, reinforcement, extending thinking and practice when working with students.

1. *Introduce topic*

We have learned a great deal about motivation, reinforcement, extending students' thinking and practice. Now let's look at a film and see how these principles are used in practice sessions in mathematics.

2. *View film "Helping in Mathematics"*

If the film is shown on television, suggest the participants may wish to jot down notes to help them recall examples. If you are showing the film you may wish to stop it to discuss examples. If the film is not available, this meeting can be used to recall previous content and apply it to classroom situations or the group leader can schedule some "live" demonstrations of helping students.

3. *Lead discussion*

Discuss examples from the film and from the participants' experience in using these principles when helping a child in mathematics at home and at school. Make sure you model all the principles as you accept and dignify the contributions and extend the thinking of the participants.

Discuss and clarify additional examples. Encourage participants to volunteer classroom examples and apply what they have learned to develop additional suggestions.

4. *Assign homework*

Encourage participants to reread material in this book as well as the suggested supplemental readings.

Encourage participants to practice applying all they have learned as they work with students at school and their children at home.

Read "Helping in Reading" page 51.

HELPING IN READING
MEETING PLAN*

(The participants should have read "Helping in Reading" page 51.)

OBJECTIVE
The aide/volunteer will identify and discuss principles of motivation, reinforcement, extending thinking and practice when working with students.

1. *Introduce topic*
We have read the section on "Helping in Reading" which suggested ways we might assist students with words they don't know as well as help them understand what they read. We are going to watch a film which shows students being assisted in reading. Afterwards we will discuss these techniques and develop ways each of us might use them as we work with students.

2. *View film "Helping in Reading"*
If the film is shown on television, suggest the participants may wish to jot down notes to help them recall examples. If you are showing the film you may wish to stop it to discuss examples. If the film is not available, this meeting can be used to discuss and model ways of helping students in reading or the group leader can schedule a "live" demonstration.

3. *Lead discussion*
Discuss examples from the film and from the participants' experience in using these principles when helping a child in reading at home and at school. Make sure you model all the principles as you accept and dignify the contributions and extend the thinking of the participants.

Discuss and clarify additional examples. Encourage participants to volunteer classroom examples and apply what they have learned to develop additional suggestions.

4. *Assign homework*
Re-read "Helping in Reading" page 51 of this book.

Encourage participants to reread previous material in this book as well as the suggested supplemental readings.

Encourage participants to practice applying all they have learned as they work with students at school and their children at home.

---

*This meeting may be combined with the next one in a two hour meeting.

HELPING IN READING

These are some suggestions for the aide/volunteer who is helping a student develop sight vocabulary and fluency in reading.

If a student is missing more than 2-3 words on a page, that book is too difficult for him to use in learning to read. The book may be used as a book about his interests but should not be used for reading instruction because he won't be able to learn so many unknown words at one time. Your task is to help him learn each word he doesn't know so he will recognize it the next time he comes to it.

Here are a few suggestions for working with students for whom reading is difficult.

A. *HELPING WITH UNKNOWN WORDS*

1. To be sure the student is *looking* at the unknown word, either you or he point to it or you or he state the name of the letter it begins with. This is not to help him with the sound but to make sure he is looking at the right word.
2. Give him a little time to think while you wait quietly.
3. If he needs help with the word, determine whether you will a) use meaning clues or b) tell him the word or c) use phonic clues.

   a. *Use meaning clues.* Figuring out unknown words from the meaning of the rest of the sentence is probably the most useful skill to develop independent reading. Have the student skip the unknown word and read the rest of the sentence. If the student reads in a hesitating way ("He-is-too-big--enough") meaning may not be apparent so you need to reread aloud what he read, giving it full meaning ("He is *too* big enough").

      If he reads the rest of the sentence and still can't figure out the word, you should read the sentence saying the initial sound of the word missed. "He went to the store w_____ his mother." If he can't supply the word with this help, you should supply it. Then have the student reread the sentence to make sure he has the practice of saying it correctly.

      You can supply other meaning clues. If he doesn't know the word "calf" you might say, "It's what we call a baby cow." You might use gestures to convey the meaning of an unknown word "He flew very _____" (raising your hand in the air for "high").

      You might ask a question which the unknown word will answer, ("Where was he going to show his calf?" At the *fair*.)

      Sometimes it is helpful to use the unknown word in a sentence about the student, "I'll bet you're *ready* to tell me that word," or to write the unknown word in a sentence with the student's name. "Darryl is *ready* to read." Then have the student read the sentence, telling him the unknown word if necessary. Afterwards, he can recall that sentence if he forgets the word.

   b. *Tell him the word.* If it is a difficult word that doesn't have obvious phonic or meaning clues (such as gnu, ceiling, whether, enough, their, etc.), say it for him. Then have him reread the sentence that contains the word so he has the practice of saying

51

it correctly when he sees it between other words. At the end of the page, go back to that word to be sure he knows it.

c. *Use phonic clues.* The student's present knowledge of phonics determines how much he can use phonics with unknown words. Initial consonants are the easiest clues but make sure you are thinking of the correct sound, (/k/ as in kitty, kite, etc., not "kuh," /r/ as in run, rate, etc., not "err").

Ask the student, "Do you know the sound of _____?" If he does, then ask, "What do you think that word would be?" If he doesn't know, you read the sentence making the appropriate beginning sound of the unknown word so he also has the help of meaning. "He caught the b(all)." Always have him reread the sentence containing the unknown word and go back to that word at the end of the page to make sure he remembers it.

Rhyming words often help. You *write* a rhyming word the student knows (so the student can see as well as hear the similarity). "What is this word?" (write "cat") "Then what would it be if it started with an 'f'?" Write "fat" *under* the word "cat" so the student can see both words.

Vowels are much more difficult. The ability to supply the correct sound depends on whether a student has had successful instruction with simple and complex vowels. Usually it is safer to tell him the word rather than have him "spit and sputter" through it. Make sure he reads the sentence that contains the word and that you go back to that word so he knows he is accountable for remembering it.

B. *HELPING WITH UNDERSTANDING*

If a student has read in a hesitating way, with pauses to figure out words, it is hard for him to get meaning from what he has read. You can help him by:

1. Rereading a sentence with your voice giving maximum meaning. "That's right, 'Bill was really worried about the pony'."
2. Asking the student to reread a sentence or a paragraph. "Now reread this and you'll see you know all the words."
3. You read a paragraph or a page aloud and ask the student to be your teacher. Stop on an occasional word and have him supply it. In this way he can hear it read with maximum meaning, he can practice following with his eyes while the words are read (this will speed up his eye movements) and he can practice saying the words which he needs to practice. If he has missed a word previously, stop on that word so he can practice by saying it.
4. Check his comprehension with questions about what happened in the story. If he has trouble answering a question, direct him to the page where the answer can be found. If he can't find it, direct him to the correct paragraph. If he still can't find the answer, ask him to read the first sentence aloud to see if the answer is there. Continue to the next sentence until he finds the information.

C. *HELPING WITH RETENTION OF WORDS LEARNED*

1. Watch for later occurrence of the word missed to see if it is read correctly.
2. Refer to words missed as "that word that puzzled you" *not* "the word you didn't know," the former is dignified, the latter demeaning.

3. Go back to unknown words (at end of page, paragraph or story, whichever is appropriate), and check to make sure the student now knows the word. If he doesn't, have him reread the sentence that contained the word and then go back to it again later. If it is remembered in the practice session, be sure to go back to it the next day to ensure its retention.

4. Record unknown words in a student's individual vocabulary booklet with the page number on which the word occurred. Have him become responsible for checking those words with you the next time you work with him. Also record the page numbers where he knew every word so he knows how many times he is successful. Occasionally review all the words in his booklet so he will retain them.

THE AIDE IN THE CLASSROOM
MEETING PLAN

(This final meeting should be used for any necessary review and to make plans for later evaluation and feedback. Additional inservice meetings may be scheduled at this time. A meeting on retention is suggested (page 60) as it provides an excellent review of many important principles necessary to "aide-ing in education." If possible, it is desirable that the principal or representative of the administration be present for final questions and assignments.)

OBJECTIVE
The aides/volunteers will discuss their role and responsibilities in the classroom.

1. *Introduce topic*
We have learned a great deal about helping in the classroom. In this film we will see the many things an aide/volunteer can do when "aide-ing in education." Afterwards we will discuss your role and responsibilities as a member of the educational team in this school.

2. *View film "The Aide in the Classroom"*
If the film is shown on television, suggest the participants may wish to jot down questions they want to raise after the film. If you are showing the film, you may wish to stop for discussion at certain points. If the film is not available, discuss suggested responsibilities of aides/volunteers, page 56.

3. *Lead discussion*
The discussion should focus on concerns and questions of the participants. When questions and issues are outside the realm of aides/volunteers they should be referred to the school administration. ("That is certainly a matter of concern. Let's refer it to the principal for (s)he has the authority and information to deal with it.") Examples of such issues are personality conflicts, curricular questions, school policies, routines and schedules, etc.

In the discussion stress the necessity for systematic communication between aide/volunteer and teacher. Refer to page 58 for suggestions and ask participants for other ways they might suggest that would be convenient and successful.

4. *Plan for evaluation and future meetings*
Set a future date and explain the procedure for aides/volunteers evaluating the usefulness of their training (suggested evaluation form page 68). Make them aware that teachers will also be evaluating the workshop. Alert them to the need for feedback as to what modifications should be made in future workshops and the importance of additional content suggestions which they are in the best position to make.

5. *Conclude workshop series*

(Should the decision be made to have the meeting on retention as part of the workshop series, this should be done at the conclusion of that meeting.)

Point out that these workshop sessions have been only the beginning of learning about ways to increase students' learning. The participants must now assume the responsibility for translating this knowledge into their own work in the classroom. Suggest that they may wish to schedule additional meetings. (Plans and content for a meeting on retention is on page 60.) Emphasize that much of the information they have learned was formerly intuitive and has only recently been articulated so it could be systematically taught. Consequently, while teachers are using many of the techniques in their classrooms, they may not be familiar with some of the terms used in this workshop. By working together, aide/volunteer and teacher can augment and extend the effectiveness of each other in a truly productive partnership for the benefit of youth.

Respond to final questions.

Terminate workshop with "appreciation and best wishes."

SUGGESTED AIDE/VOLUNTEER
RESPONSIBILITIES

How teachers can best use aides/volunteers is determined by the competency of the aide/volunteer, the needs of the students, and by the creativity of the teacher. To determine responsibilities appropriate for your particular situation, it may be helpful to look at four categories of possible teacher assistance.

1. Housekeeping
2. Clerical Work
3. Record Keeping
4. Working with Children

Some responsibility for assisting in each of these categories makes a more interesting assignment. To enrich and extend the learning in your classroom, a teacher should plan opportunities where the aide/volunteer can share her unique skills and talents: musical, culinary, artistic, scientific, needlework, crafts, and even collections from buttons to stamps. Be creative, but be sensitive to the needs of your teacher, aide/volunteer, students and yourself.

Following is a check list of possible responsibilities for aides/volunteers, to which you will add the particular assignments needed by your classroom:

Preparation and Housekeeping

_____ Make teaching aides, such as games, flashcards.

_____ Set up for learning activities.

_____ Prepare materials, such as cutting paper, sharpening pencils.

_____ Straighten and replenish supplies that are low.

_____ Maintain art supplies by washing paint brushes, filling water containers, (mixing paints, clay, etc.).

_____ Prepare milk, juice or snack.

_____ Help to care for plants, animals.

_____ Clean areas as needed: shelves, table tops, counters, sink.

Clerical

_____ Prepare dittos and stencils.

_____ Run duplicating machines.

_____ Operate audio/visual equipment.

_____ Type as needed.

_____ Make phone calls as needed.

_____ Secure films and books from storage.

_____ File materials.

_____ Put names of children on roll, lists, materials, notes.

_____ Correct students' papers (using model prepared by teacher).

Record Keeping

_____ Record attendance.

_____ Record behavior of children.

_____ Record children's work.

_____ Collect and record milk money, lunch money, etc.

_____ Inventory as needed.

Working with Children

In small groups and/or one to one:

_____ Practice in math, reading spelling, writing.

_____ Write and/or type dictated stories.

_____ Talk with children for their language practice.

_____ Read stories.

_____ Sing with children.

_____ Play an instrument with children.

_____ Assist with a cooking or other hobby experience.

_____ Supervise a learning center.

_____ Assist with an art experience.

_____ Supervise a listening center.

_____ Help a group move from one place to another, such as classroom to lunchroom, library, auditorium.

_____ Play/teach games in classroom and on play yard.

_____ Share hobbies, interests and collections.

In large groups:

_____ Read a story.

_____ Monitor children working on assignments.

_____ Accompany group on field trips.

_____ Assist class in library.

_____ Supervise lunchroom.

_____ Supervise play yard.

_____ Assist at dismissal, with crossing guard, etc.

SUGGESTIONS FOR TEACHER
AIDE/VOLUNTEER COMMUNICATION

Communication between teacher and aide/volunteer is essential for a successful program. Much can be accomplished in informal conversation but systematic and planned "talks" should be scheduled. In this way teacher and aide/volunteer can benefit from the knowledge and experience of the other.

Usually a short weekly conference before school, during recess, at lunch or after school will accommodate the needs for direction and feedback.

Many teacher—aide/volunteer teams find it also helpful to communicate in writing.

One way teacher and aide/volunteer can communicate when there is no time for a conference, is through a notebook. Below is a sample of one notebook communication used successfully. Routines were established in writing and specific duties listed daily. Note that aide/volunteer and teacher "talk" via this notebook.

This sample on the next page is just one way to communicate in writing. Try designing your own. You'll find it is a good record of what has been accomplished and what needs to be done.

Teacher—Aide/Volunteer Notebook

Daily Routines

Check Supplies:
   pencils for sharpening
   paste jars for filling
   paper supply
See basket for papers to be filed.
On Counter:
   Children's work to be filed.

Before you leave:
   Check learning centers to see
   that all needed materials are there.
   Place name cards in pocket chart
   ready for tomorrow.

October 3
You will take small group for practice in writing
numerals. Set up on round corner table.

Music teacher comes today - you can use this
time for getting supplies ready for tomorrow.

Will need more brads for the booklet
project.

October 4
Math practice group again!

I left folder with practice results on your
desk.
10:30 Small group - as identified yesterday - to
library with you.
Something is bothering Jane. She was
quite withdrawn. I didn't get to her.

RETENTION (Optional Meeting)
MEETING PLAN

(Review and clarify content from previous meeting)

OBJECTIVE

The aide/volunteer will state the five factors that promote retention and cite examples of use and abuse of each.

1. *Introduce topic*

We have learned there are four questions we must always consider when we practice. Let's review them briefly.

The way something is practiced makes a great deal of difference in how well it is remembered. We are going to view a film that reminds us of the importance of practice. The film also tells us about four other factors that affect remembering or retention of what is learned. You are already familiar with most of them.

2. *View film on Retention*

If the film is shown on television, suggest the participants may wish to jot down each factor as it is introduced. If you are showing the film, you may wish to stop it after each generalization is presented and have a short discussion for clarification. Have examples ready from your own experience or from the book *Retention Theory for Teachers*. If the film is not available, teach the content or have the participants read the section on page 61 before the discussion.

3. *Conduct discussion*

List the five generalizations on the chalkboard. Stress that the participants' past learning in this workshop will transfer to help them remember the five factors that promote retention. Point out that the participants learned about pleasant feeling tone in motivation theory and they know how to use positive reinforcement. Both produce feelings that promote memory. The degree of original learning is related to how meaningful something is and how efficiently it is practiced. Encourage participants to discuss their classroom experiences and/or problems related to retention. Indicate that the book *Teach For Transfer* will give them more information about transfer.

If the techniques for "making mistakes productive" were not discussed in the last meeting they may be included here. Role playing different ways of responding to an incorrect answer is a vivid way of demonstrating ways of working with children. Role playing also provides models of many different ways to accomplish the same result.

During discussion stress the possibilities for use of motivation, reinforcement and retention whenever the aide/volunteer is assisting a learner with practice. Give examples and use these strategies as you lead the discussion.

4. *Assign homework*

Read section on retention on page 61.

Read *Retention Theory for Teachers* if it is available.

Try these techniques at home and at school.

60

RETENTION

The ability to remember what has been learned has always been a desired outcome of teaching. Until recently, however, it has been assumed that certain people had "good" memories and others didn't. Now we know that the way something is taught has a great deal to do with how well it is retained and whether it can be recalled for use at a later time. Consequently, it is important to identify the things a teacher/aide/volunteer can do, as well as the things the student *should* do to change "never heard of it" to "sure I remember!"

There are five factors that each teacher/aide/volunteer should try to build into every learning session if students are to remember what they learn. Those factors are: 1) meaning, 2) degree of original learning, 3) presence of feeling tone, 4) schedule of practice, and 5) transfer.

1. *MEANING*

The more meaningful the material, the better the retention.

Meaning is one of the most important, yet often neglected factors that increases students' remembering what they have learned. When material is meaningful it is learned faster and remembered longer. Meaning does not exist in the material, it is a result of the relationship of the student's past experience to the material which is to be learned. For example, the meaning of the word confused is enhanced by "Bill was confused when his team started using a completely different set of rules" because students have experienced the confusion created by different rules.

In contrast, unless the student has had a great deal of experience in science, meaning is not helped at all by the sentence, "The conflicting data confused the scientist."

The teacher/aide/volunteer should relate whatever is being learned to something the student already knows or has experienced so the new material becomes more meaningful to that student. Meaningless material is as difficult to learn and remember as a list of nonsense syllables would be. Real words, from his experience, may be longer and more complex than nonsense syllables but they are easier to learn because the student knows what they mean. The same number of words becomes even more meaningful, are learned more easily and remembered longer when they are put together in a sentence that tells something about the student. "Remember how confused we were when we tried to figure out that new game?"

Number combinations should be put into word problems that are about the student, the class, or something interesting the student has experienced. ("Suppose you spend $.45 for lunch each school day, how much would you spend in a week?") Information about important events and people also should be related to the experience of the student. ("If you were in Daniel Boone's party, when you woke up this morning you would have _____.") Geographic information should if possible, be translated into terms the student understands. (That means if you started driving now it would take you until _____ to get there.) All of these statements are illustrative examples, not the exact words or situations you should use.

2. *ORIGINAL LEARNING*

The greater the degree of original learning, the better the retention.

Anything that is not well learned is rapidly forgotten. Think about your own memory for names after you have met a person or a group of people only once. You have no trouble remembering the name of the president of the United States even though you have never met him. Of course the president has a great deal of meaning for you but also you learned his name well when he was campaigning and you have seen him or heard his name on television many times since.

"The better the original learning the better the retention" reminds us that anything worth teaching should be taught well, not just "once over lightly." Make sure the student really knows and understands what he is learning before you move on. So he won't become tired or bored with doing the same thing over and over, vary the examples and the way he is working. ("Now I'll do one and you tell me if it is right." "I'll reread that page while you follow so you can say the next word when I pause.")

If it is obvious that the activity needs to be changed or if time runs out, come back to that same learning the next time you work with the student so you know the degree of his original learning is sufficient and he will be more apt to remember what he has learned.

To achieve an adequate degree of original learning of the principles and techniques described in this booklet, we suggest you go back and reread each section as you practice using these ideas with students. After only one reading, you will be more apt to forget the principles or to remember them incorrectly.

3. *FEELING TONE*

The presence of feelings, either pleasant or unpleasant aids retention.

How you feel about something effects how well you will remember it. Think of one of the best dinners you ever had. It's easy to think of several isn't it? Now think of an awful meal. Usually the memory is only too vivid. Now try to remember what you had for dinner a week ago today. Unless something unusual happened to give that day particular meaning, you'll have a hard time remembering it unless the meal was very good or very poor.

Your memory of those meals is a practical application of how feelings, either pleasant or unpleasant aid memory. We try to make learning pleasant so students will remember. We are careful about making learning unpleasant because, while that learning may be remembered, the student may avoid that particular learning in the future. Think of an unpleasant class you may have taken. You remember it well because of your unpleasant feelings don't you? You may have learned the material in that class but you also learned to avoid that subject from then on. You don't want this to happen to the students you work with so by all means make the feelings in the learning situation pleasant. If you must make them a little bit unpleasant to let a student know he needs to get started or to finish, make sure you return to pleasant feeling tones so he will remember the material with pleasure. ("You need to stay in until you can write these words correctly: ... Good for you, I knew you could learn them quickly.") Students should remember school as a pleasant place where learning was fun.

Neutral feeling tones, where learning is neither pleasant nor unpleasant mean that learning (like a so-so meal) may soon be forgotten. Sometimes you will make feelings neutral by saying, "Don't worry about it today" because the student is tired or frustrated and you know that if you work any longer it may become unpleasant. But *you* remember that you must come back to that material at a later time and then you need to make the learning experience pleasant so the student will learn the material and it will be better remembered.

4. *PRACTICE*

The way something is practiced affects how well it is remembered.

You have already learned the answers to the four questions which guide effective practice: How much? How long? How often? and How well? These answers should guide the activity any time you practice with a student or expect him to practice with others or by himself.

Remember that "intending to remember" and "practicing remembering" by saying it or writing it again and checking correctness is one of the best ways of ensuring remembering. Tests can become effective, highly motivated practice sessions because students usually try very hard to remember on a test. If you remember that tests should be an aid to helping students remember rather than an attempt to "catch them" forgetting, you will make tests pleasant, non threatening and use them so students find out how much they have learned. Tests also identify for students the things they have forgotten so you and they can focus their learning effort on material not yet learned rather than practicing something they already know well.

5. *TRANSFER*

Past learnings can transfer into the present and assist or interfere with learning.

When a past learning assists a student with a present learning, we say the transfer is positive. Positive transfer is occurring when a student who remembers the word "want," easily learns "wants" and "wanting." We help this positive transfer take place when we emphasize the *similarity* of the three words.

When a past learning interferes with a present learning we say the transfer is negative. Negative transfer is occurring when a student reads "want" for "went." We say he has forgotten "went." We try to keep negative transfer from occurring by not teaching things together when they are apt to become confused because they are similar. "One thing at a time" is a good motto for improving retention. Should confusion occur we need to emphasize the *difference* in the two learnings. ("This word _e__ would be "went." This word, _a__ would be want.")

The skilled teacher/aide/volunteer is constantly thinking about what a student already knows or has experienced that would help him with his present learning (positive transfer) and future remembering. This is why relating new learning to a student's past experience is helpful as well as enhancing the meaning of that new material. It is also important to think about previous learning that might confuse the student or cause him to forget so that negative transfer can be minimized or eliminated.

If you wish to know more about how to use transfer theory to help your students learn quickly and remember well, we'd suggest you read *Teach For Transfer*. TIP Publications.

Bibliography

Hunter, Madeline. *Retention Theory for Teachers*. TIP Publications, P.O. Box 514, El Segundo, California 90245. 1967.

Hunter, Madeline. *Teach for Transfer*. TIP Publications, P.O. Box 514, El Segundo, California 90245. 1971.

SAMPLE LETTER TO PARENTS*

Dear Parents:

    We are pleased to announce that a special series of ten meetings** will be provided for those parents who wish to work with us as school aides and volunteers.

    These meetings are designed to increase the skills of all of us as we work with children so they will learn more, learn it faster and develop better work habits. At the meetings we will develop our skills in how to affect children's motivation to learn, how to increase their learning, to stretch their thinking, and help them practice more productively. Participants will learn practical ways to use these skills whenever they are with children at school and at home.

    Meetings will be held for five Thursday mornings from _____ to _____ a.m. beginning __(date)__. This program has special personnel and materials so enrollment will be limited to the first 30 parents who return the attached slip.

_____
Principal

_____
Aide/Volunteer Chairperson

*************************************** (tear off) ***************************************

I am able to attend all five meetings. Please enroll me in the series.

_____
Name

*This is a *sample* letter. The principal or chairperson should add correct dates, times and rewrite anything that would make it more appropriate for local recipients.

**Schools may wish to shorten this to a series of five meetings of approximately 2-2½ hours each.

Sample Bulletin to the Teacher

FIRST AID FOR CLASSROOMS—
THE AID YOU'VE WISHED FOR

You are about to receive what you've always wished for—an extra pair of hands to help, another set of eyes to see and ears to listen, another allotment of patience, more assistance for your students, another adult with whom you can share ideas and perceptions, in short an extension of "you" to help bring off what your head and heart wish to accomplish in your classroom.

Your aide/volunteer really is an extension of "you" for your plans and your skill will direct her actions. She is not a teacher so she will look to you for guidance in what you wish her to accomplish.

Your aide/volunteer comes to you with skills and knowledge, some of which she only recently acquired. As a result there may be words and lables that are different from those that were used when you learned your teaching skills. Read the booklet *Aide-ing in Education* to acquaint yourself with the vocabulary that was used in her training. By doing this, the two of you can communicate with ease. The skills she has been taught are described in that book so you may know what you can expect from her when she works with children. You also will find a procedure for systematic communication and a list of suggested ways you might use your aide/volunteer so there truly is an extension of you. Teaching her your classroom routines related to rules, procedures, materials and equipment will enable her to function as effectively as possible.

In addition to the skills she has learned, you should find out the special talents your aide/volunteer possesses that may be different from yours. When you use those talents they add richness to your classroom. You will also need to help her become acquainted with the children so she shares your perceptions and is accepted and respected by them.

Because your aide/volunteer has had only a few hours of training, she will need to look to you as a model who practices with children the things she has been taught in her training course. That training was designed to help her increase learning and improve student behavior by the use of the principles of motivation, reinforcement, practice, retention and extending thinking. She will come to you having had the opportunity to acquire the following competencies: (page 10 of this book).

After you work with her, you will be asked to make suggestions for her future inservice training.

There are some suggestions of ways she might help you on page 56.

SCHOOL AIDE/VOLUNTEER WORKSHOP
TEACHERS' EVALUATION FORM

Name _____

Date _____ Grade Level _____

(1) Did you request volunteers? _____ Yes _____ No

(2) What responsibilities did you assign to volunteers?_____

_____

(3) Number of aides/volunteers that work in your classroom? _____

_____

(4) Number of aides/volunteers that have taken inservice workshop? _____

_____

(5) Did they seem prepared to work with children? _____ Yes _____ No

(6) Did they seem prepared to work with you? _____ Yes _____ No

(7) Did they talk to you about the skills they had learned? _____ Yes _____ No

(8) If "yes" what were some of the things they discussed?

(9) What seemed to be their greatest strengths?

(10) What were some of the skills they lacked?

(11) What would you recommend be added to their traning?

(12) Was any of thé content in their training unnecessary?

(13) List any problems that arose:

(14) Do you wish volunteers in the future?

(15) Additional comments:

WORKSHOP PARTICIPANTS EVALUATION FORM

Name _____

Teacher _____

Date _____ Grade Level _____

(1) Approximately how many hours per week do you volunteer? _____

(2) What workshop sessions have been most helpful in the classroom? Check.

_____ motivation   _____ extending thinking   _____ practice

_____ reinforcement   _____ story reading

(3) What other skills have you needed that should be included in the workshop sessions?

_____

(4) Check any area of workshop content that you had not had an opportunity to use.

_____ motivation   _____ extending thinking   _____ practice

_____ reinforcement   _____ story reading

(5) Suggestions for improvement of aide/volunteer program in your school.

(6) What do you like best about being a volunteer?

(7) What do you like least?

(8) What additional help do you need from the teacher and coordinator?

(9) Would additional workshop meetings be useful? _____ What suggestions do you have for future meetings?

SUPPLEMENTAL READING

Hunter, Madeline. *Motivation Theory for Teachers.* TIP Publications, P.O. Box 514, El Segundo, California 90245. 1967.

_____. *Reinforcement Theory for Teachers.* TIP Publications, P.O. Box 514, El Segundo, California 90245. 1967.

_____. *Retention Theory for Teachers.* TIP Publications, P.O. Box 514, El Segundo, California 90245. 1967.

_____. *Teach More—Faster!* TIP Publications, P.O. Box 514, El Segundo, California 90245. 1969.

_____. *Teach for Transfer.* TIP Publications, P.O. Box 514, El Segundo, California 90245. 1971.

Hunter, Madeline, and Carlson, Paul V. *Improving Your Child's Behavior.* TIP Publications, P.O. Box 514, El Segundo, California 90245. 1967.

FILMS

1. Welcome Back to School
2. Increasing Motivation
3. Increasing Productive Behavior
4. Motivation and Reinforcement in the Classroom
5. Extending Students' Thinking
6. Reading a Story to Extend Thinking
7. Improving Practice
8. Helping in Math
9. Helping in Reading
10. The Aide in the Classroom
11. Retention

Special Purpose Films
26740 Latigo Shore Drive
Malibu, California 90265
(213) 457-7133